# A BRIDGE OF BOOKS

# A BRIDGE OF BOOKS

*From the collection of the Yiddish Book Center*

*A Bridge of Books*

White Goat Press, the Yiddish Book Center's imprint
Yiddish Book Center
Amherst, MA 01002
whitegoatpress.org


Printed in the United States of America at The Studley Press, Dalton, MA
10 9 8 7 6 5 4 3 2 1

Paperback ISBN 979-8-9886773-6-9
Hardcover ISBN 979-8-9886773-7-6

Library of Congress Control Number: 2023917516

Book and cover design by Michael Grinley

# INTRODUCTION

These forty-nine books, on display in the Yiddish Book Center's core exhibition *Yiddish: A Global Culture*, represent a journey into the modern Yiddish imagination. Yiddish readers were voracious in their curiosity and hungry for news of the world around them. Here you will find books about polar exploration, the life of gauchos and ostrich farmers, the origins of Islam, the Spanish Civil War, and Norse legends. The genres include politics, social science, memoirs, poetry, children's stories, travel writing, reportage, fantasy, literary classics, guidebooks, scientific writing, and musical theater. A cornucopia of Yiddish literature, these books reflect the practical concerns as well as the hopes and dreams of a migrant people.

Each of these volumes has been donated by friends and supporters of the Yiddish Book Center—a tiny sample of the million-plus books that the Center has received since 1980. They include some real rarities: *Yapanishe mayselekh* (*Japanese Tales*), a slim pocket book of Japanese stories; *Khine* (*China*), an impressively comprehensive guidebook cum statistical primer; and *Kavkazer libe* (*Love in the Caucasus*), a Yiddish theater operetta script. All are found in just two or three other collections worldwide.

The Arabic-Yiddish manual—"a practical method to acquire in a month the spoken Arabic of Palestine and Egypt"—is an intriguing example of another remarkable manifestation of Jewish modernity: the explosion of language primers for Yiddish speakers in the nineteenth and twentieth centuries. In addition to Arabic, these include English, Esperanto, Spanish, Polish, Russian, Hebrew, French, and German.

While some of these forty-nine titles are translations of world classics, most are original Yiddish texts. Of these, one or two at most have been translated. Sadly, that too is representative. Despite the exciting surge of new translations in recent years, the vast majority of Yiddish books—numbering somewhere between 40,000 and 60,000 titles, including outstanding works of fiction and nonfiction—remain inaccessible to all but the relatively small number of Yiddish readers.

—David Mazower

*Chief curator and writer,* Yiddish: A Global Culture,

*the Yiddish Book Center's new core exhibition*

# PLATES

# Dertseylungen fun Oystralye

## (Tales from Australia)

P. GOLDHAR (1901-1947), MELBOURNE, 1939

Author Pinchas Goldhar emigrated from Poland to Australia in 1928, where he became editor of the first Yiddish newspaper in Melbourne. In *Tales from Australia*, Goldhar describes the experiences of Australian Jews struggling to acclimate to new surroundings.

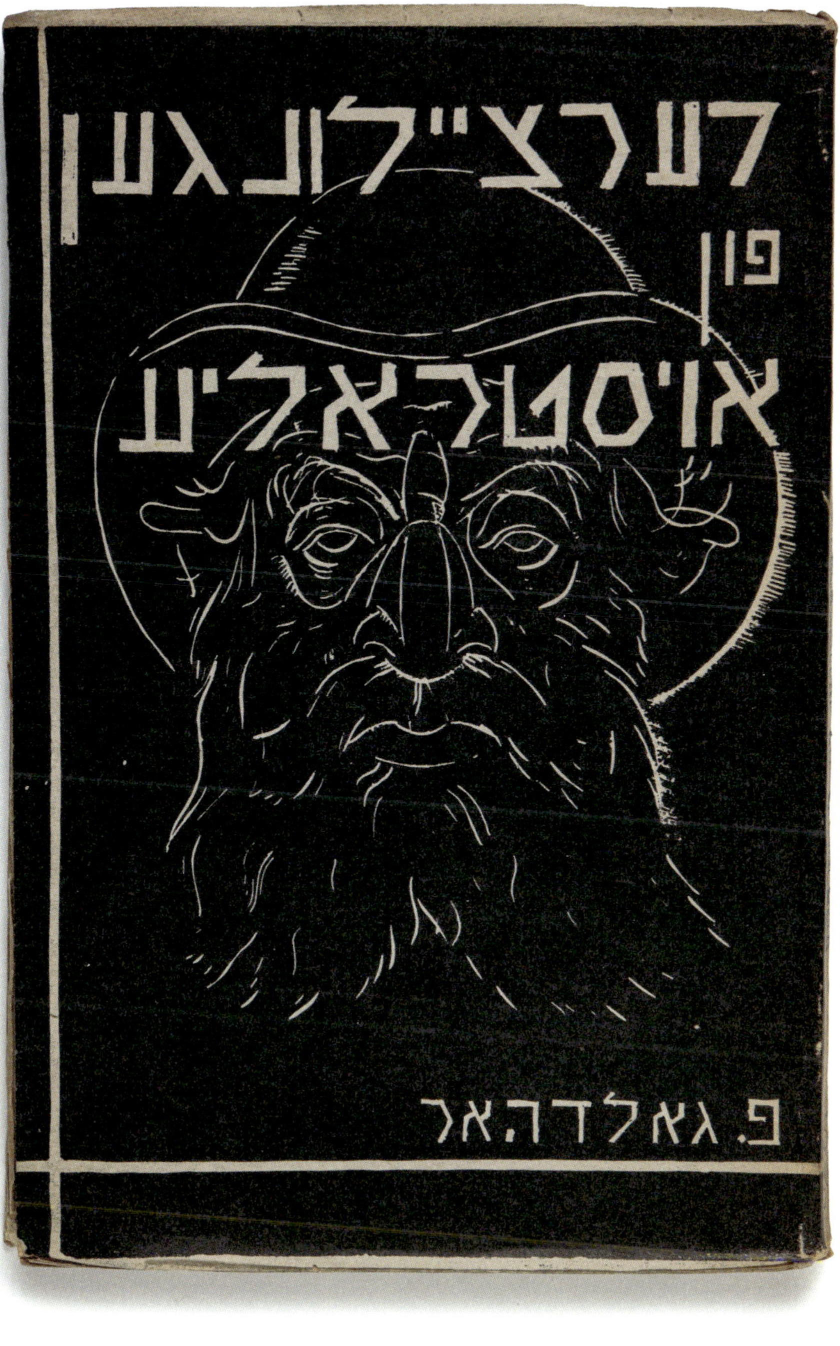
דערציילונגען
פון
אויסטראליע
פ. גאלדהאר

## GELEBT UN GEKHOLEMT IN OYSTRALYE

(Lived and Dreamed in Australia)

ISAAC NACHMAN STEINBERG (1888-1957), MELBOURNE, 1945

A prominent activist for the Socialist Revolutionary party in Russia, I. N. Steinberg served as justice commissar in Vladimir Lenin's first coalition government. In the 1930s and '40s he traveled to Australia to promote a potential Jewish settlement in the remote Kimberly region. With its kangaroos on the front cover, this book details Steinberg's experiences down under.

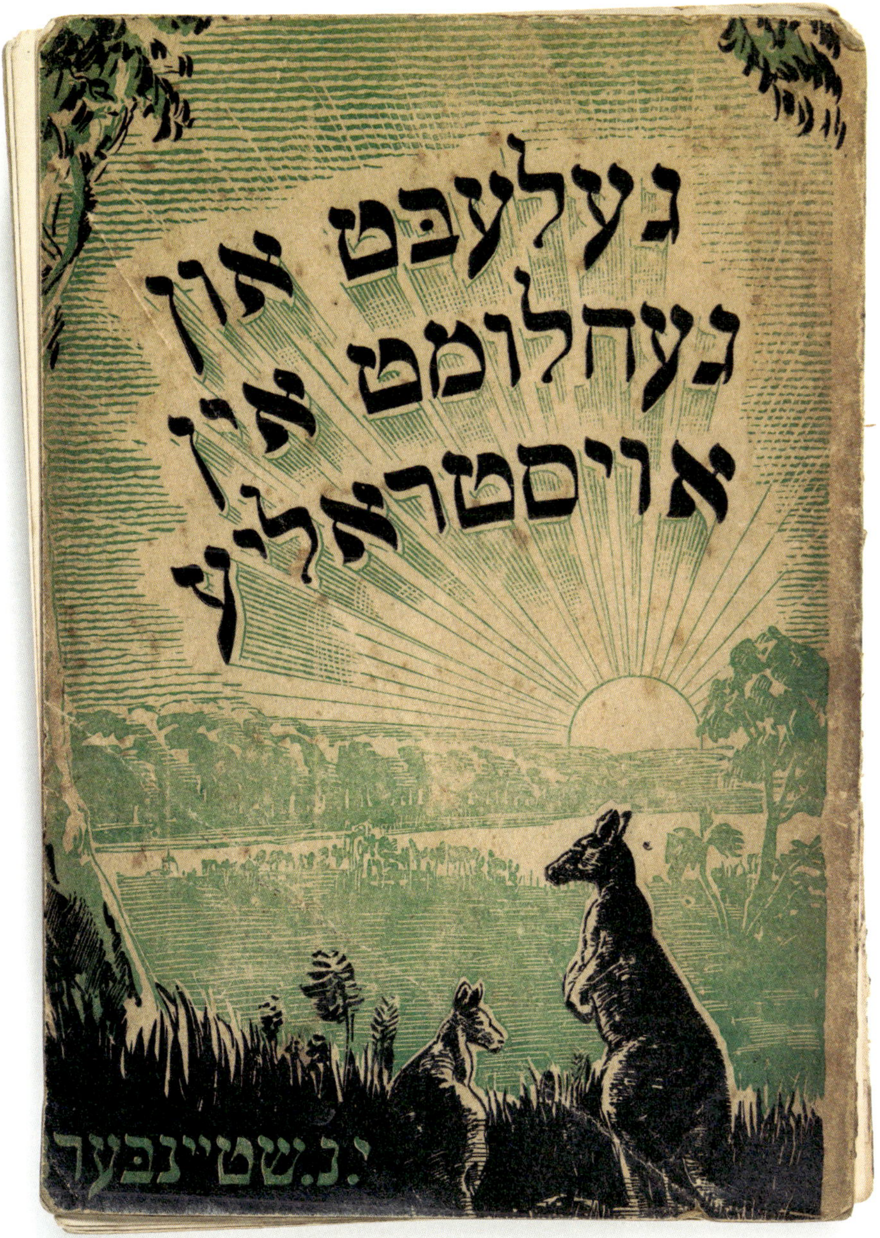
געלעבט און
געחלומט אין
אויסטראַליע
י. נ. שטיינבערג

## AMERIKE
(America)

SHLOYME SHVARTS (SCHWARTZ) (1907-1988), CHICAGO, 1940

This book cover features iconic symbols of the United States, such as Abe Lincoln and the Stars and Stripes, and contrasts them with depictions of two archetypal Americans from across the racial divide. For better or worse, the modernist typeface announces, America is the land of the future. Schwartz, an immigrant to the United States from Poland, made his home in Chicago, where he published extensively in journals and anthologies.

שלמה שווארץ

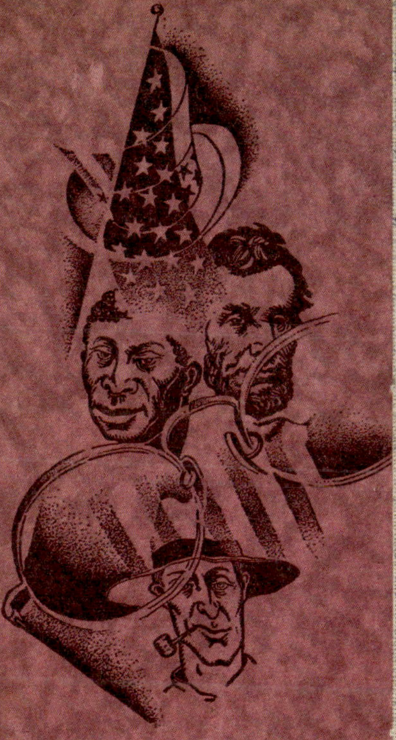

אמעריק

# IN LAND FUN RASN-DISKRIMINATSYE

(In the Land of Race Discrimination)

Y. LEKHTER (?-?), WARSAW, 1953

The powerful, full-color cover image and chapter titles like "Contemporary Slavery" and "Ghettos in All American Cities" leave little doubt about this book's content and perspective. Writing in Warsaw in the early 1950s, Lekhter, about whom very little is known, aims his pen at the stark racial injustices in postwar America.

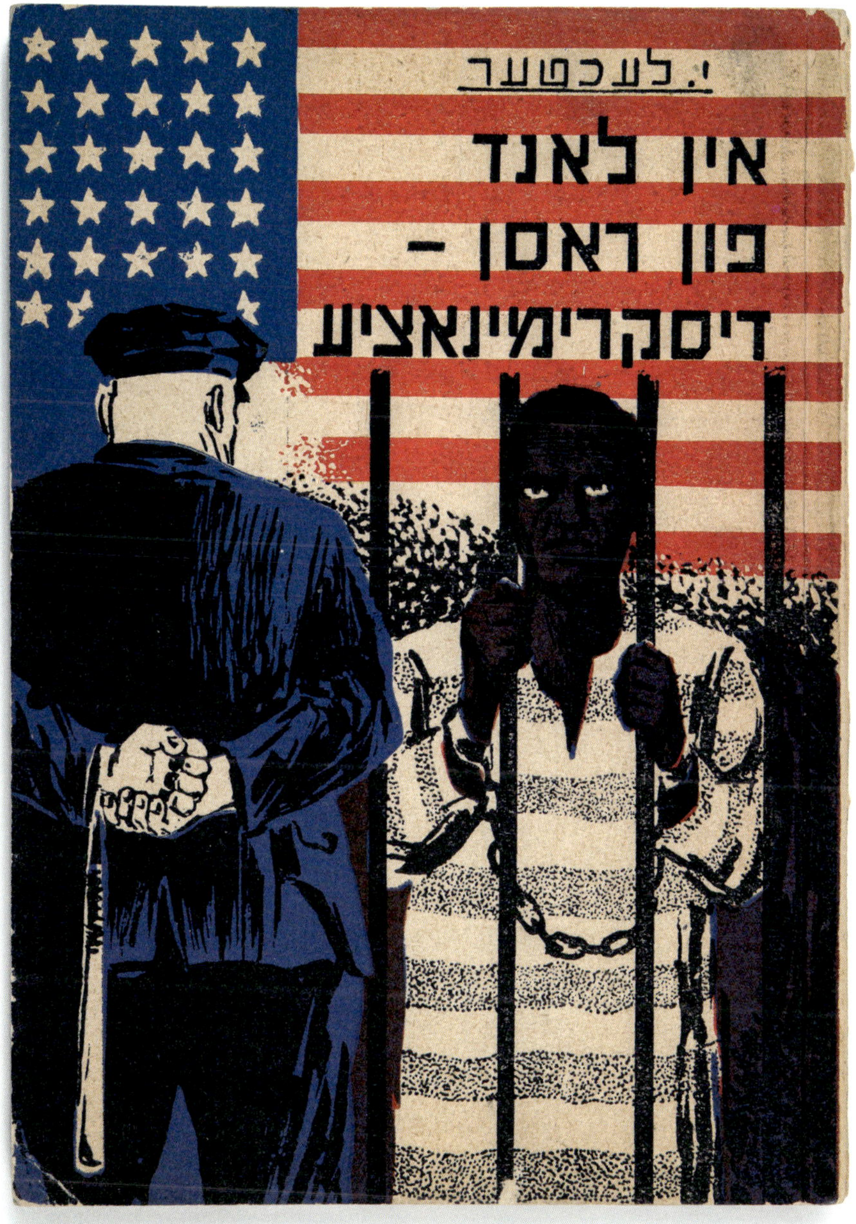
י. לעכטער
אין לאנד
פון ראסן –
דיסקרימינאציע

## Ver greyt pogromen af yidn in Amerike?

(Who Is Plotting Pogroms against Jews in America?)

JOHN SPIVAK (1897–1981), NEW YORK, 1934

The oversize question mark stretching across the cover signals this volume's investigative focus. The author, John Spivak, was a reporter known for his communist leanings and his writings on issues such as racial justice and antisemitism. This book, an investigation of anti-Jewish violence in interwar America, is a Yiddish translation of articles he first wrote for the leftist publication *New Masses*.

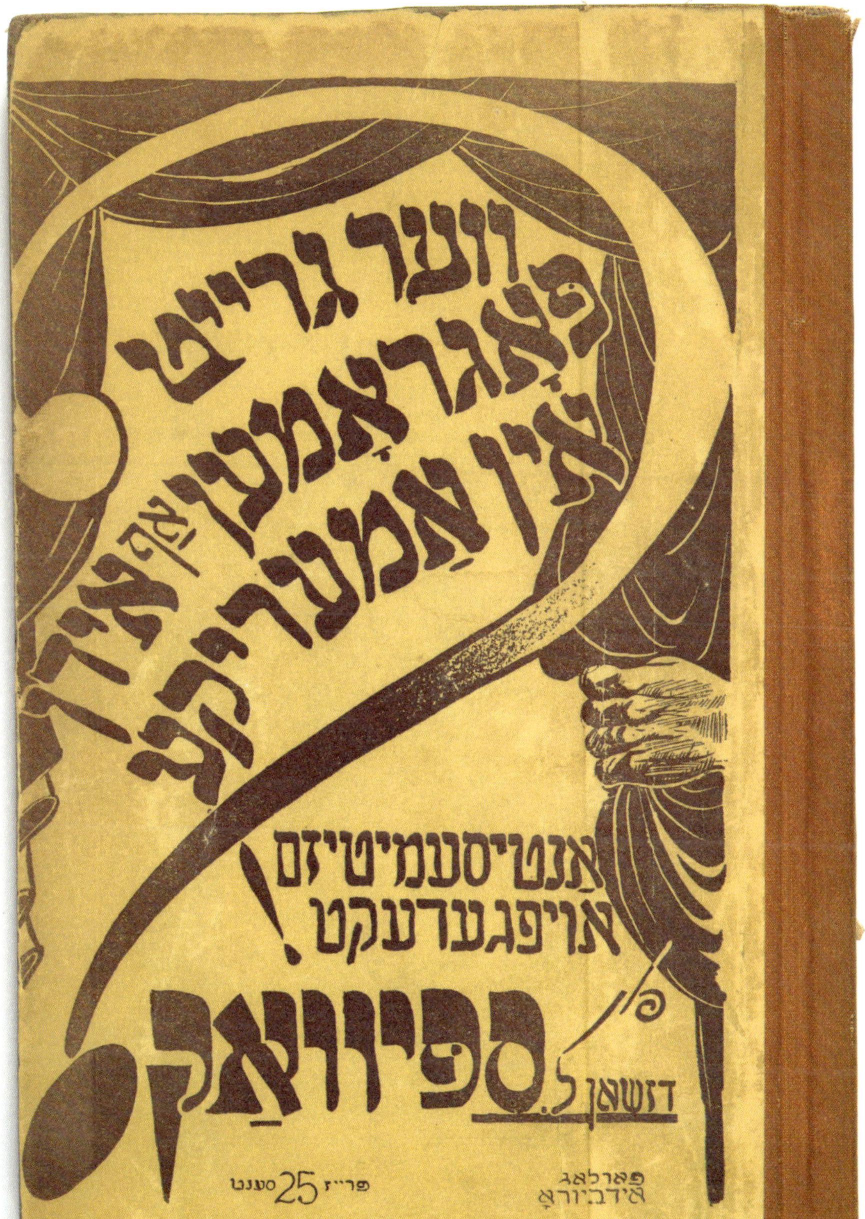
ווער גרייט פאָגראָמען אויף אידן אין אמעריקע?
אַנטיסעמיטיזם אויפגעדעקט!
פון
דזשאָן ל. ספּיוואַק
פרייז 25 סענט
פאַרלאַג
אידביוראָ

## INGELE, RINGELE

(Little Boy, Little Ring)

LEON ELBE (LEON BASSEIN) (1879-1928), NEW YORK, 1929

The fantastical cover of this book invites readers into a magical world full of wonder and surprise, as the author writes on the title page. Depicted on the red horse is the titular boy, who travels the world with his magical ring. The story was originally serialized in the American Yiddish periodical *Kinder zhurnal* (*Children's Journal*) before being collected in this volume.

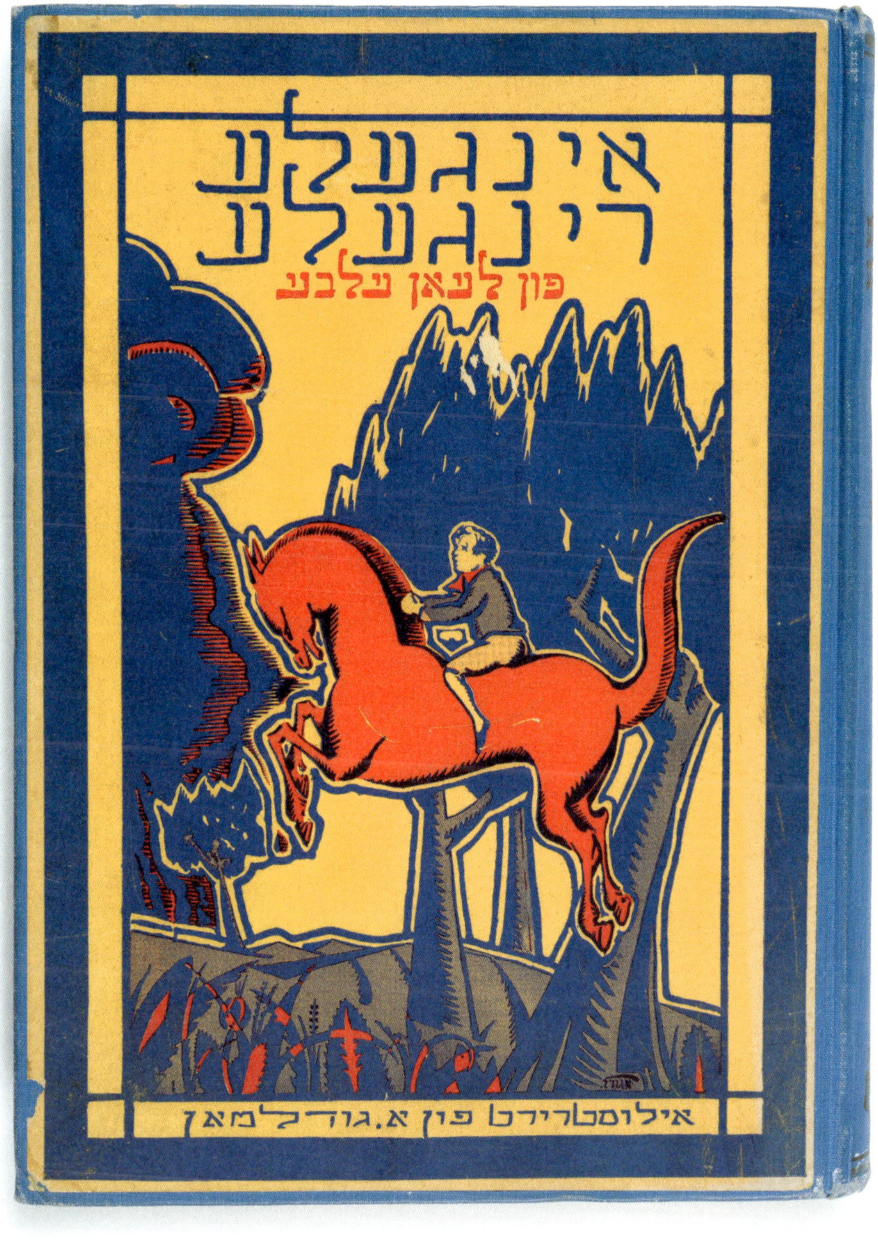
אינגעלע רינגעלע
פון לעאן עלבע
אילוסטרירט פון א.גודלמאן

# Dos lebn fun Ema Lazarus

(The Life of Emma Lazarus)

Y. B. BEYLIN (1883-1961), NEW YORK, 1946

Most notable for her poem "The New Colossus," which is engraved on the Statue of Liberty, Lazarus was born into a prosperous family, where her passion for poetry was encouraged. This slim, orange booklet details her biography and her outspoken advocacy for Jewish refugees.

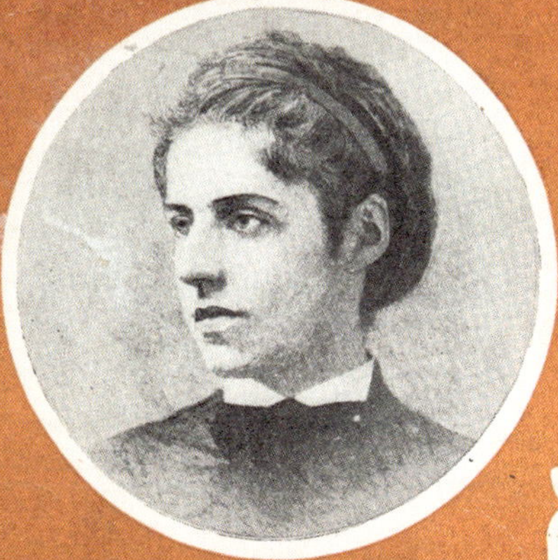

# עמאַ לאַזאַרוס

אַרויסגעגעבן פון דעם
**ביכער־פאַרלאַג**
ביים
**אידישן פראַטערנאַלן**
**פאָלקס־אָרדן**
80 פינפטע עוו., ניו־יאָרק

20¢

## AMERIKE—
## DOS LAND FUN VUNDER

(America—The Land of Wonder)

YANKEV KIRSHENBOYM (1885-1946), WARSAW, 1939

Set in bold red text above a skyline featuring Manhattan's first skyscrapers, *America—The Land of Wonder* presents the author's travels across the United States, as well as topics such as "Sandwiches—An American Food." Kirshenboym later became a Yiddish theater critic under the pseudonym Dr. Kritikus.

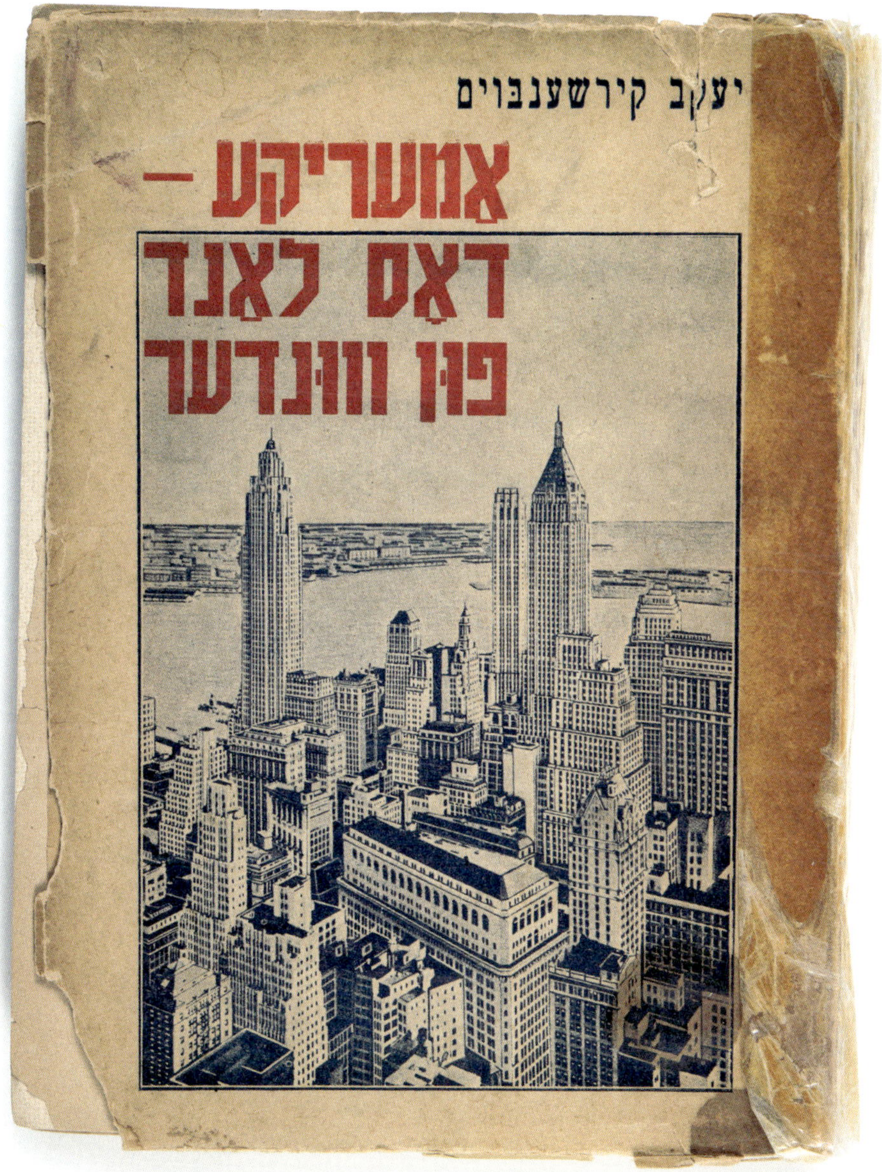
יעקב קירשענבוים
אַמעריקע –
דאָס לאַנד
פון וווּנדער

## BRODVEY UN TEL-AVIV

(Broadway and Tel Aviv)

KHONE GOTTESFELD (TUVYE SHMEYKHEL) (1890-1964), NEW YORK, 1951

As the cover illustration's contrast between burlesque stage and farmland suggests, this book chronicles Gottesfeld's multifaceted experiences as a playwright, satirist, and traveler across the length and breadth of the Jewish world. A longtime newspaper humorist and president of the Yiddish Writers Union, Gottesfeld was also known by his pseudonym, Tuvye Shmeykhl —loosely, Tobias Smiles.

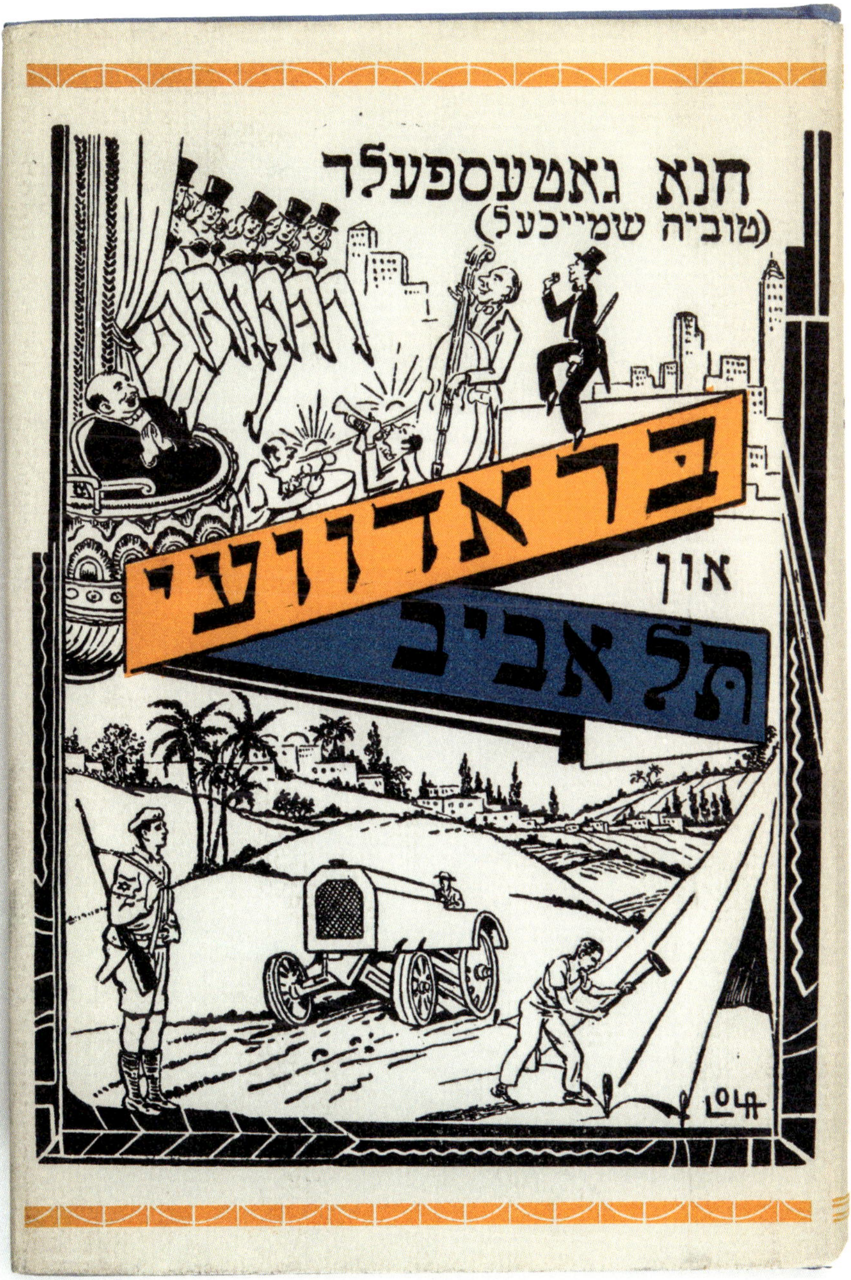

חנא גאטעספעלד
(טוביה שמייכעל)
בראדוועי
און
תל אביב
LOLA

## IN SI-GEYT BAYM YAM
(In Seagate by the Sea)

ALIZA GREENBLATT (1888-1975), NEW YORK, 1957

Greenblatt's book, with its enticing golden cover, comes already gift wrapped! Originally from Bessarabia, Greenblatt lived in Philadelphia and Atlantic City before moving to New York, and this volume's title reflects the poet's later years in the Brooklyn neighborhood of Seagate. Through her daughter, Marjorie, she became the mother-in-law of folk singer Woody Guthrie, who drew inspiration from Greenblatt and her writings.

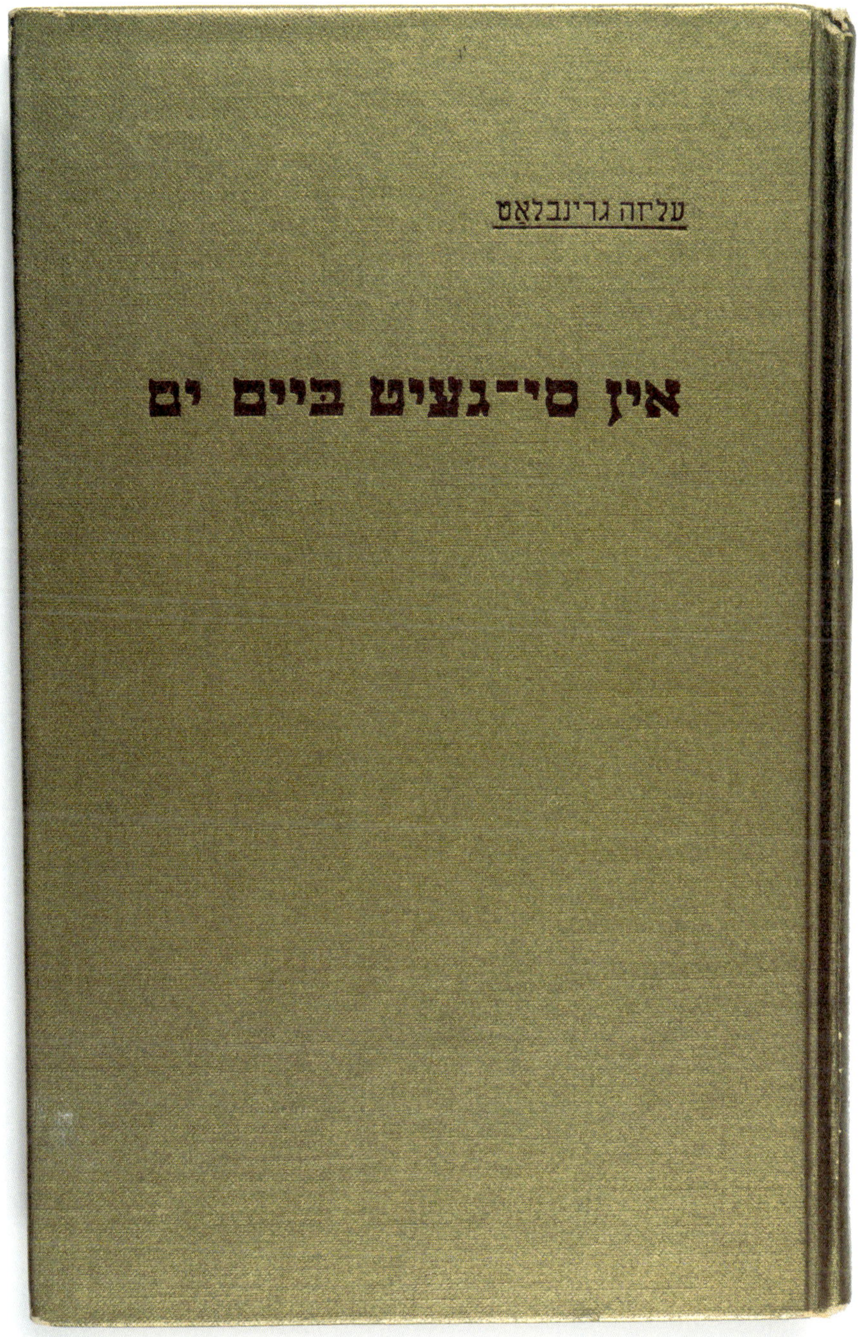
עליזה גרינבלאַט
אין סי־געיט בײם ים

## MOBI-DIK: ODER, DER VALFISH

(Moby-Dick: or, The Whale)

HERMAN MELVILLE (1819-1891)
TRANSLATED BY BARRY GOLDSTEIN (1942), MIDDLETOWN, DELAWARE, 2021

This translation of *Moby-Dick* was published as recently as 2021. The translator, Barry Goldstein, also translated J. R. R. Tolkien's *The Hobbit*, continuing the tradition of making popular classics available for Yiddish-speaking readers of all ages.

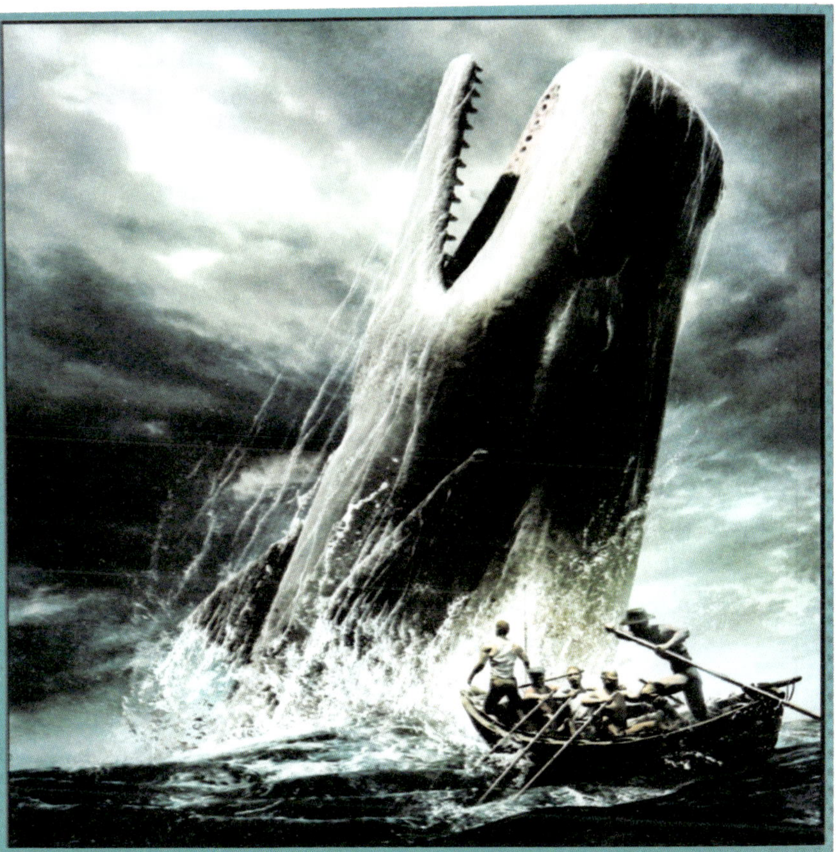

# מאָבי־דיק

אָדער

# דער וואַלפֿיש

הערמאַן מעלוויל

## DER ALTER UN DER YAM

(The Old Man and the Sea)

ERNEST HEMINGWAY (1899-1961)
TRANSLATED BY MEYER SHTIKER (1905-1983), NEW YORK, 1958

Leonard Baskin's austere portrait of Hemingway featured on the cover of this book mimics the simple yet challenging prose of its author. Meyer Shtiker, an immigrant to America from Ukraine, worked as a furrier before becoming a poet and translator of—in addition to Hemingway—Rilke and T. S. Eliot. The publisher, Israel London, was known for the elegant design of books issued through his press, *Der kval* (*The Source*).

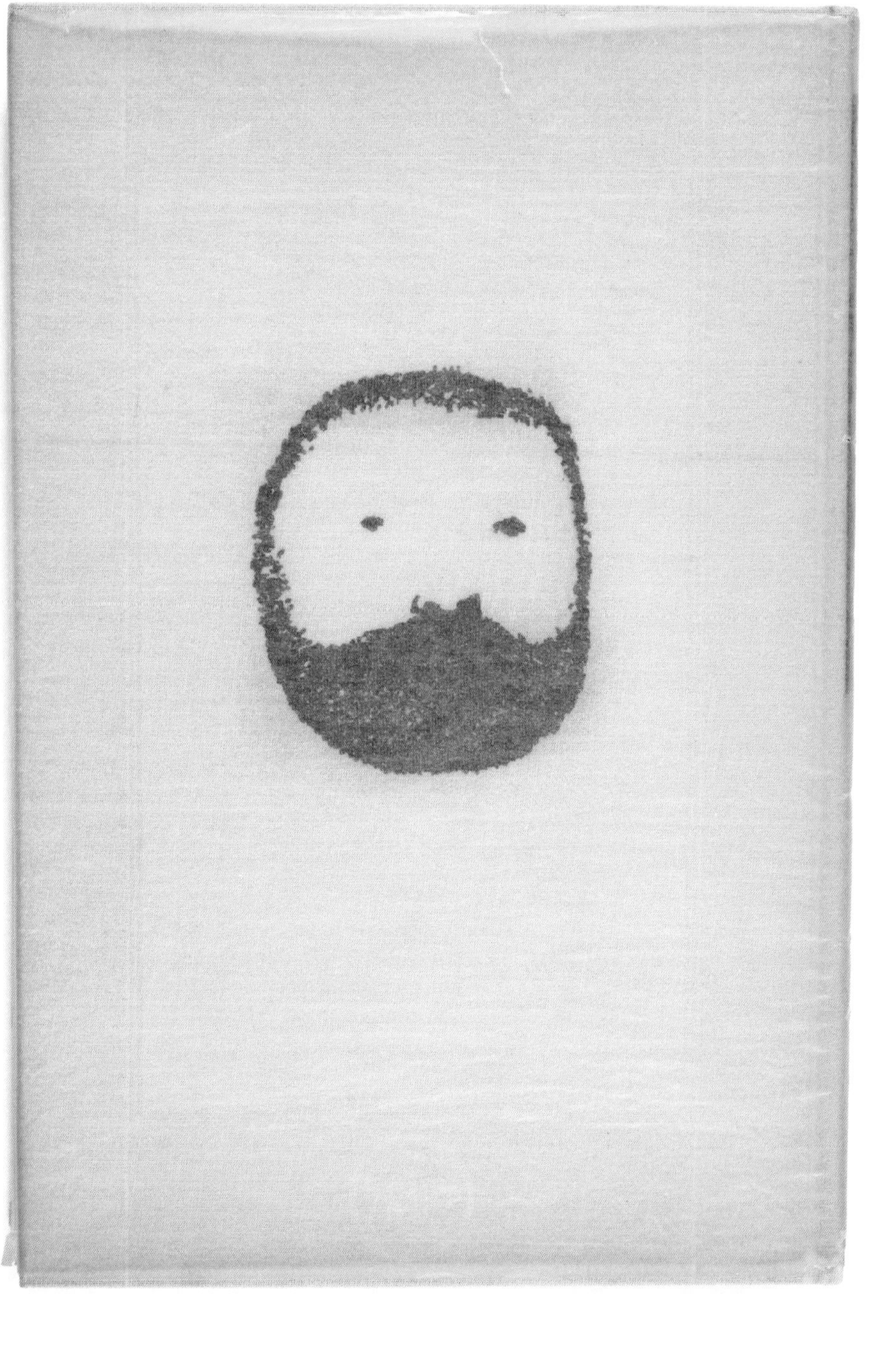

## Untern kubaner himl

(Under Cuban Skies)

Y. K. FRUMES (ITSIK KOZLOVSKI) (1898-1979), NEW YORK, 1939

Subtitled "Notes of a Jewish Tailor," this travelog from the late 1930s presents Frumes's observations on gender roles, cuisine, and the Yiddish-speaking immigrant community in Havana and rural Cuba. The tropical cover is by Note Kozlovski, a New York–based illustrator of children's books.

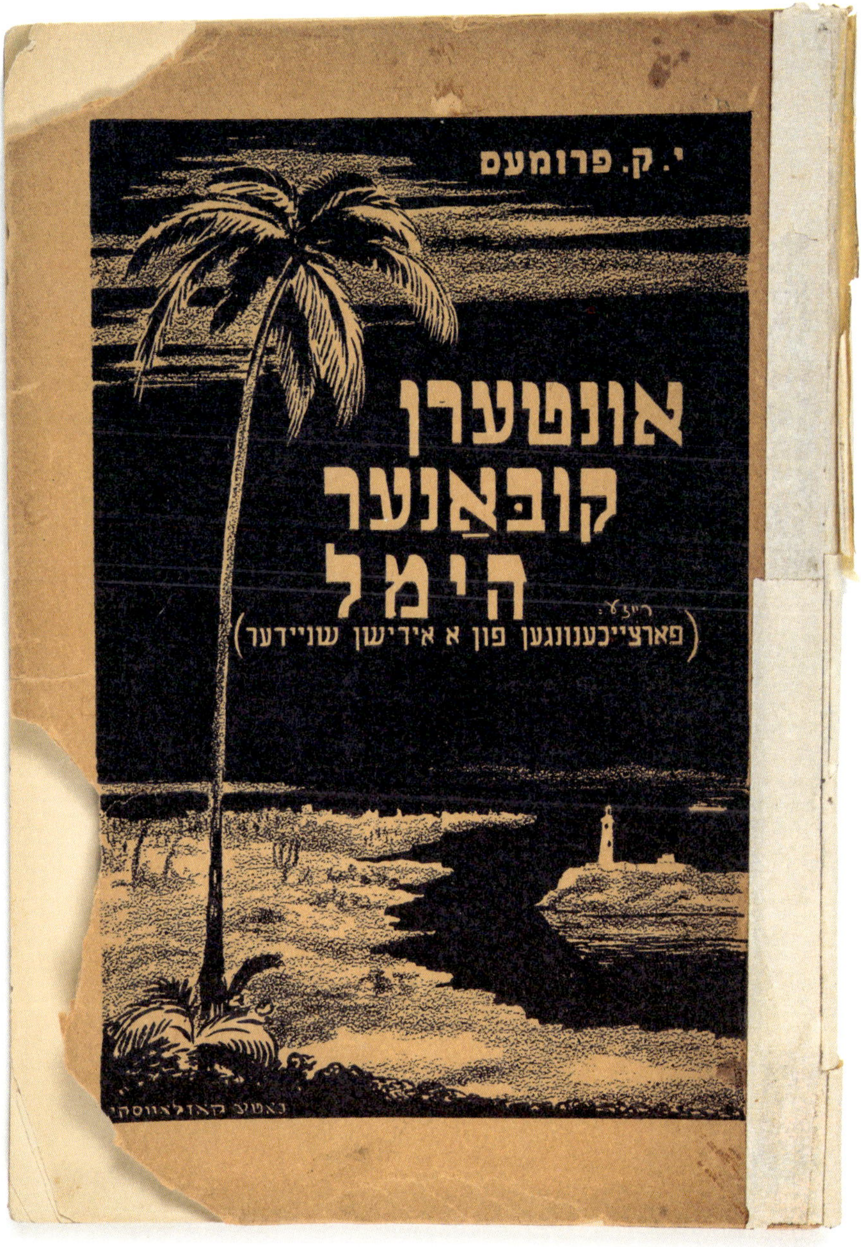
י. ק. פרומעס
אונטערן קובאַנער הימל
רייזע:
(פאַרצייכענונגען פון א אידישן שניידער)
נאטע קאזלאווסקי

## Gautshos: Geveylte dertseylungen un bilder

(Gauchos: Selected Stories and Portraits)

JAVIER DE VIANA (1868-1926)

TRANSLATED BY Y. AKSENTSOV (1888-1956), BUENOS AIRES, 1925

Gauchos, skilled horsemen of the grasslands, were South American folk heroes, like cowboys in the United States. In his translator's preface, Aksentsov asserts that the only Spanish-to-Yiddish translation before 1925 was of *Don Quixote*. With a wave of Jewish immigration to Latin America in the 1920s, Aksentsov decided to translate this popular work by the Uruguayan-born author Javier de Viana, who was exiled to Argentina during the long-running Uruguayan civil war.

# גאַוטשאָס

געוויילטע דערציילונגען
און בילדער
פון
כאַוויער דע וויאַנאַ

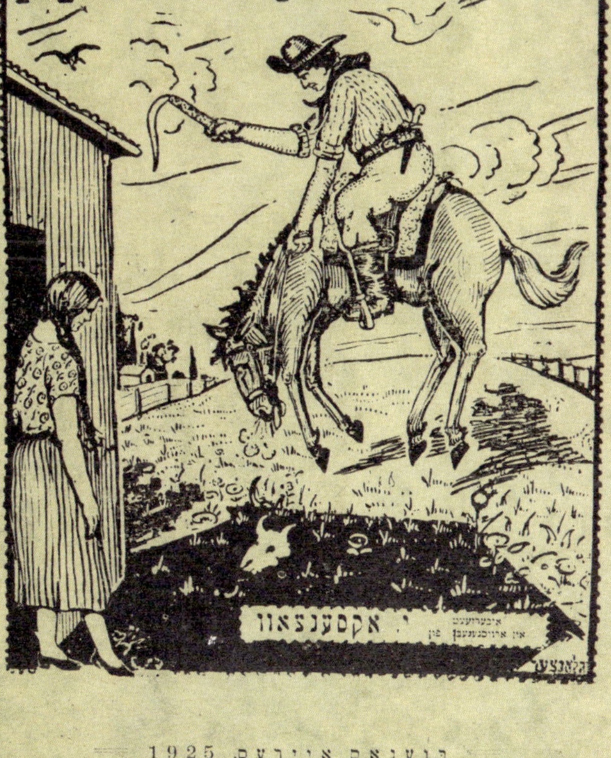

איבערזעצט און אויסגעגעבן פון י. אקסענצאוו

בוענאס איירעס. 1925

## DER LINDZHERA

(The Linyera)

MORDKHE (MARCOS) ALPERSON (1860-1947), BUENOS AIRES, 1937

The portrait on this novel's cover depicts the *linyera*, or itinerant farmer, who comes to Argentina to escape pogroms in Eastern Europe. Alperson was sent to Argentina by the Jewish Colonization Association (JCA) but became dissatisfied with the JCA's lack of hands-on agricultural knowledge. He spent the rest of his life in Buenos Aires and Mauricio, the agricultural colony he helped found in Buenos Aires Province.

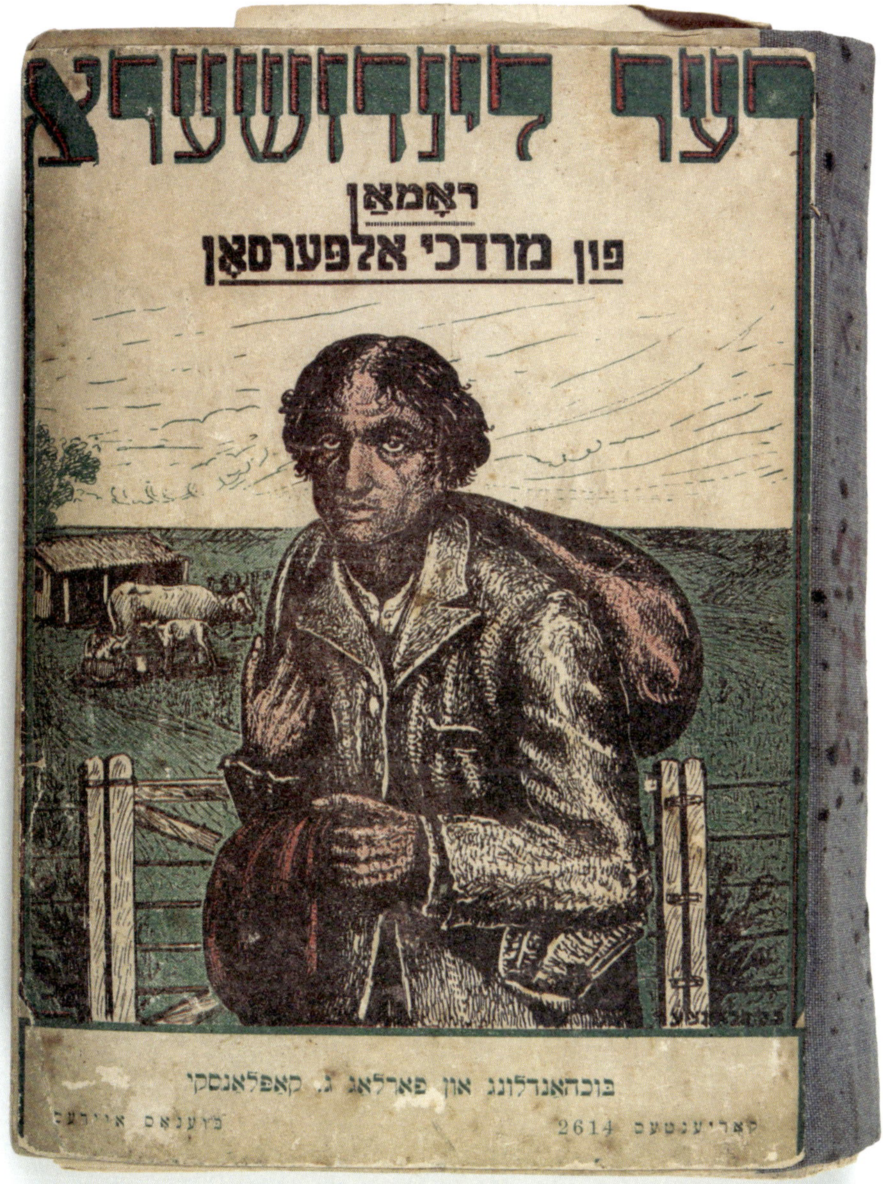
דער לינדזשערצ
ראמאן
פון מרדכי אלפערסאן
בוכהאנדלונג און פארלאג ג. קאפלאנסקי
בוענאס איירעס
קאריענטעס 2614

# FABLEN

(Fables)

KH. Y. FARBER (1889-?), BUENOS AIRES, 1936

This collection of rhyming children's fables features lively animal illustrations, Pampas grassland tales, and even a conversation in a general store between a package of tea and a barrel of yerba mate (Yiddish: *zherbe*), the national drink of Argentina. The author, Khayim-Yitskhok Farber, immigrated to Argentina as a teenager and was wildly prolific, composing over eight hundred stories for children.

# פאבלען

ה. י. פארפער

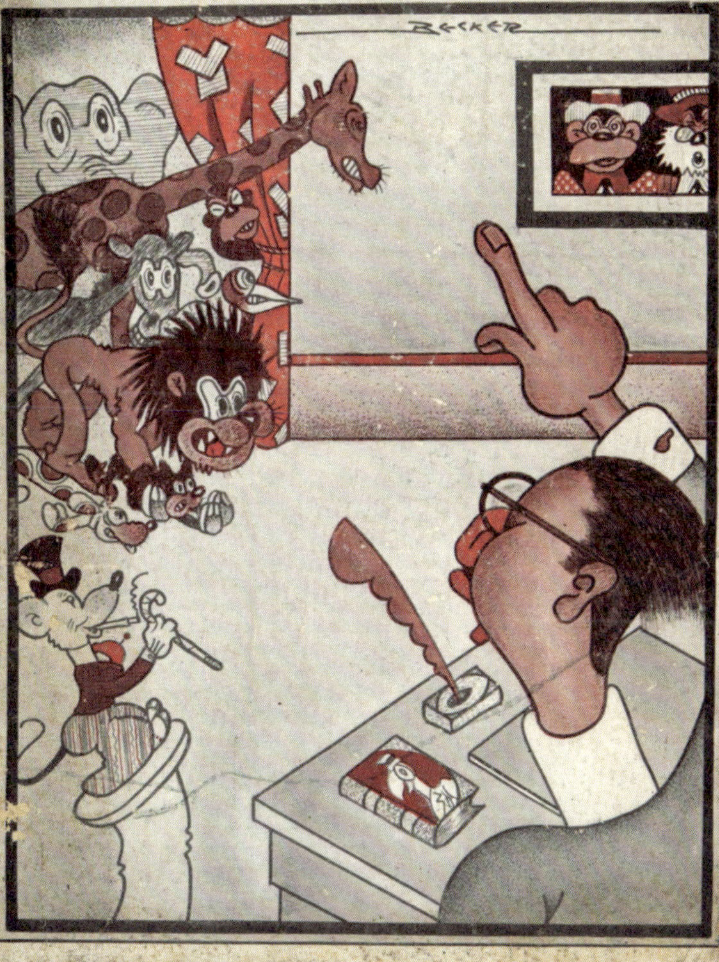


פארלאג און בוכהאנדלונג ג. קאפלאנסקי
קאריענטעס 2614 — בוענאס איירעס — 1936

## GESHIKHTE FUN YIDN IN BRAZIL

(History of Jews in Brazil)

YITSKHOK RAYZMAN (1901-1976), SÃO PAULO, 1935

Born in Sokolow Podlaski, Poland, Yitskhok Rayzman later lived in Buenos Aires, São Paulo, Detroit, and Safed, Israel. His book on the early Jewish history of Brazil focuses on Sephardic Jews who fled the Inquisition and draws on sources in Hebrew, Spanish, Dutch, and Portuguese. The ship depicted on the cover, the *Nau Bretoa*, is believed to be the first ship to transport enslaved Africans to Brazil, in the early 1500s.

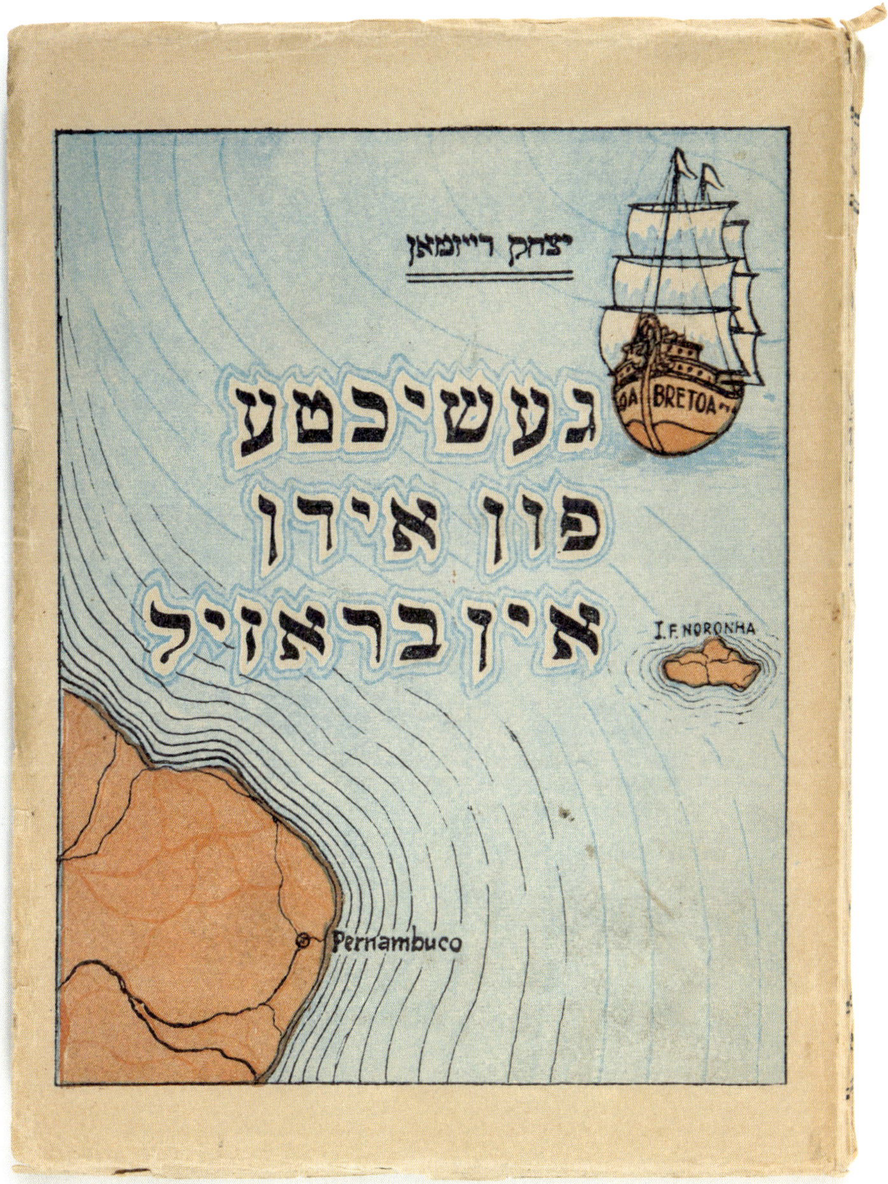
יצחק רייזמאַן
געשיכטע
פון אידן
אין בראזיל
BRETOA
I. F. NORONHA
Pernambuco

# OYDTSHORN: YERUSHOLAIM D'AFRIKE

## (Oudtshoorn: The Jerusalem of Africa)

LEYBL FELDMAN (1896-1975), JOHANNESBURG, 1940

The town of Oudtshoorn, with its feather production for the millinery trade, was known as the ostrich capital of the world. Jewish immigrants arrived there during the first ostrich boom, at the end of the nineteenth century, and established the first Hebrew school in South Africa. The boom was short-lived, and author Leybl Feldman describes dealers and exporters "feeling as mistreated as the ostriches felt after being plucked."

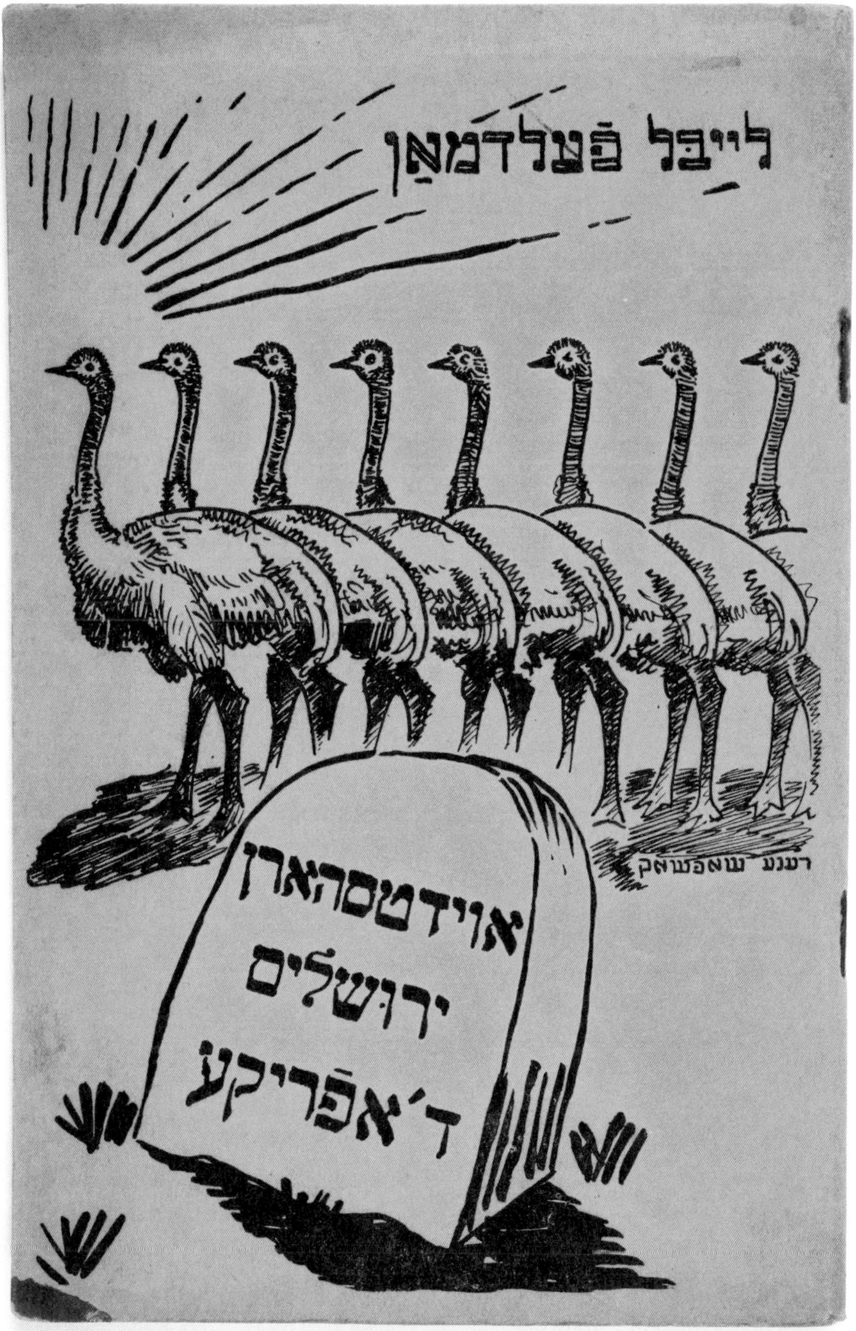

לייבל פֿעלדמאַן
רענע שאפשאק
אוידטסהארן
ירושלים
ד׳אפֿריקע

## YIDN IN YOHANESBURG

(Jews in Johannesburg)

LEYBL FELDMAN (1896-1975), JOHANNESBURG, 1956

This book uses newspaper clippings, photographs, and vital records to tell the story of Jewish settlement in Johannesburg. The cover illustration strikingly conveys the rapid urbanization of the city and the ever-present mining industry. Feldman immigrated from Lithuania and wrote many books on the Jewish history of South Africa.

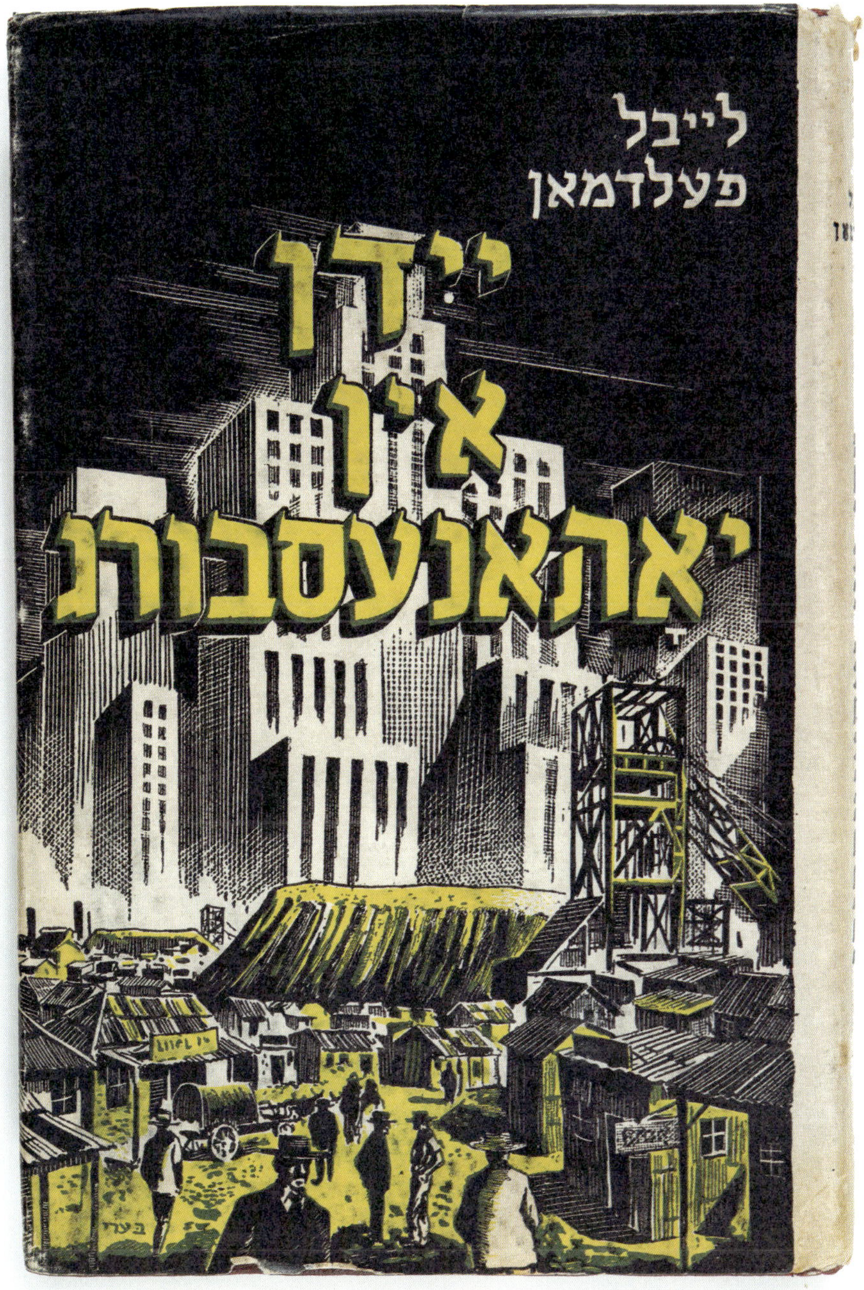
לייבל
פעלדמאן
יידן
אין
יאהאנעסבורג

## Shvarts un vays
(Black and White)

RAKHMIEL FELDMAN (1897-1968), NEW YORK, 1957

Rakhmiel Feldman (brother of Leybl Feldman) was prominent in South African Jewish organizations and the national Labour Party, where he helped establish the country's first high school for Black students. In this story collection, with cover art by painter Irma Stern, he describes Zulu culture and music, the intolerance of white society toward interracial marriage, and the exploitation of laborers in the mining industry, "where gold can be obtained at the price of Black workers' lungs."

# שוואַרץ און ווייס

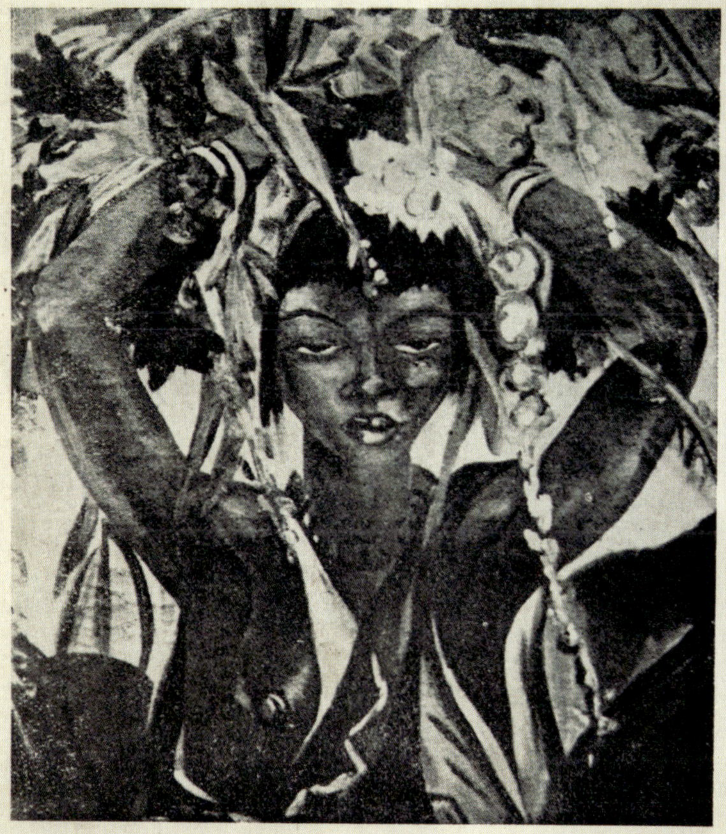

פון

רחמיאל פעלדמאַן

## Di letste nesiye

(The Last Journey)

ROBERT FALCON SCOTT (1868-1912)
TRANSLATED BY A. SHIN-RO (?-?), WARSAW, 1922

*The Last Journey* documents British naval officer Captain Scott's attempt to reach the South Pole in 1911. What began as a scientific inquiry resulted in a race between Scott and a Norwegian expedition team. Tragically, Scott and his four crew members perished while making the return journey. This account was compiled from Scott's diaries and was translated into Yiddish in 1922.

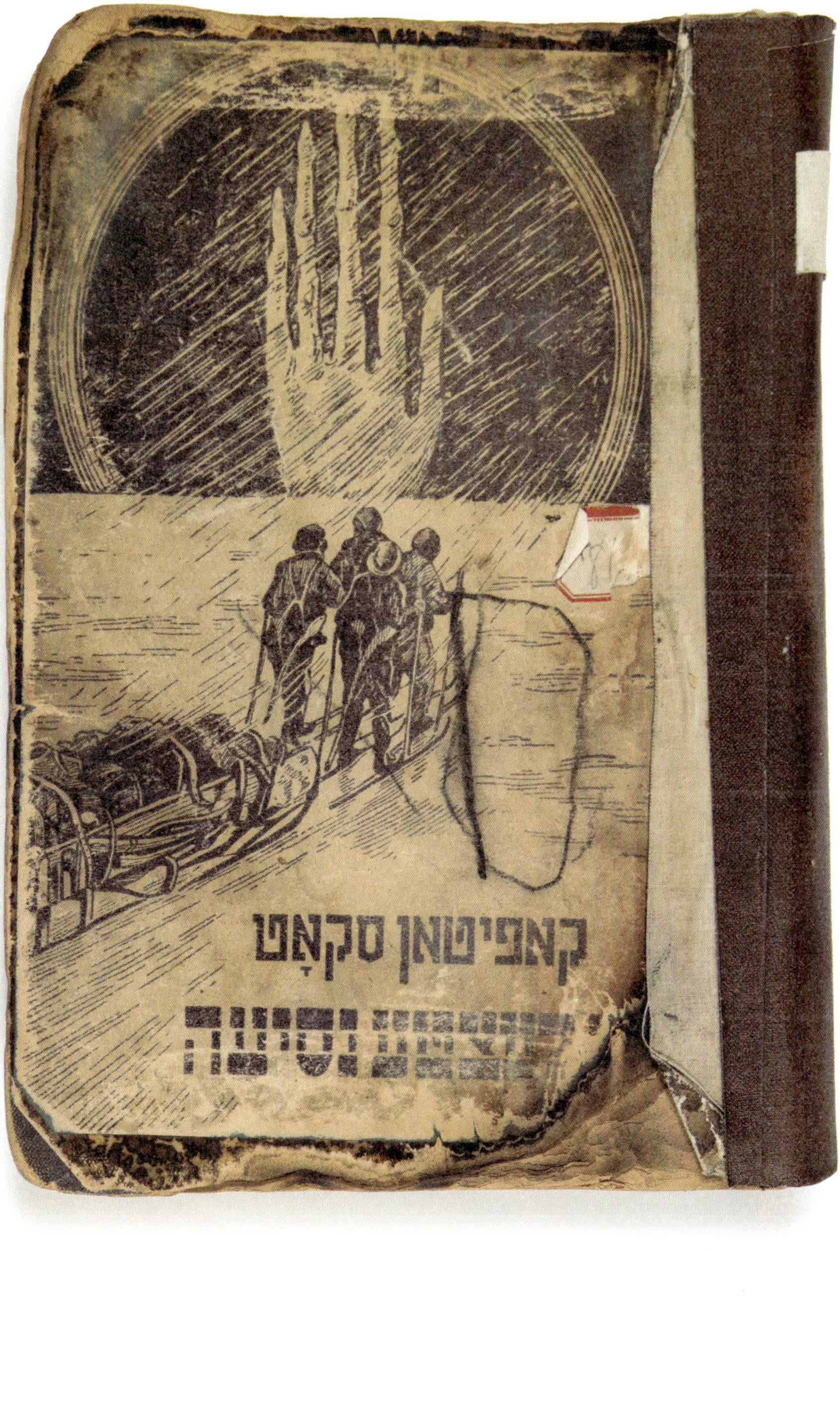
קאַפּיטאַן סקאָט

## YIDN IN SHPANISHN KRIG 1936–1939

(Jews in the Spanish War, 1936–1939)

DAVID DIAMANT (1904-1994), WARSAW/PARIS, 1967

This book details the experiences of Jewish volunteers in the International Brigades during the Spanish Civil War of 1936–1939. Author David Diamant was the secretary of the Jewish-Spanish Aid Committee in Paris and also wrote about Jews in the French resistance. The cover illustration is a detail from *Guernica*, Picasso's response to the horrors of the conflict, painted in 1937.

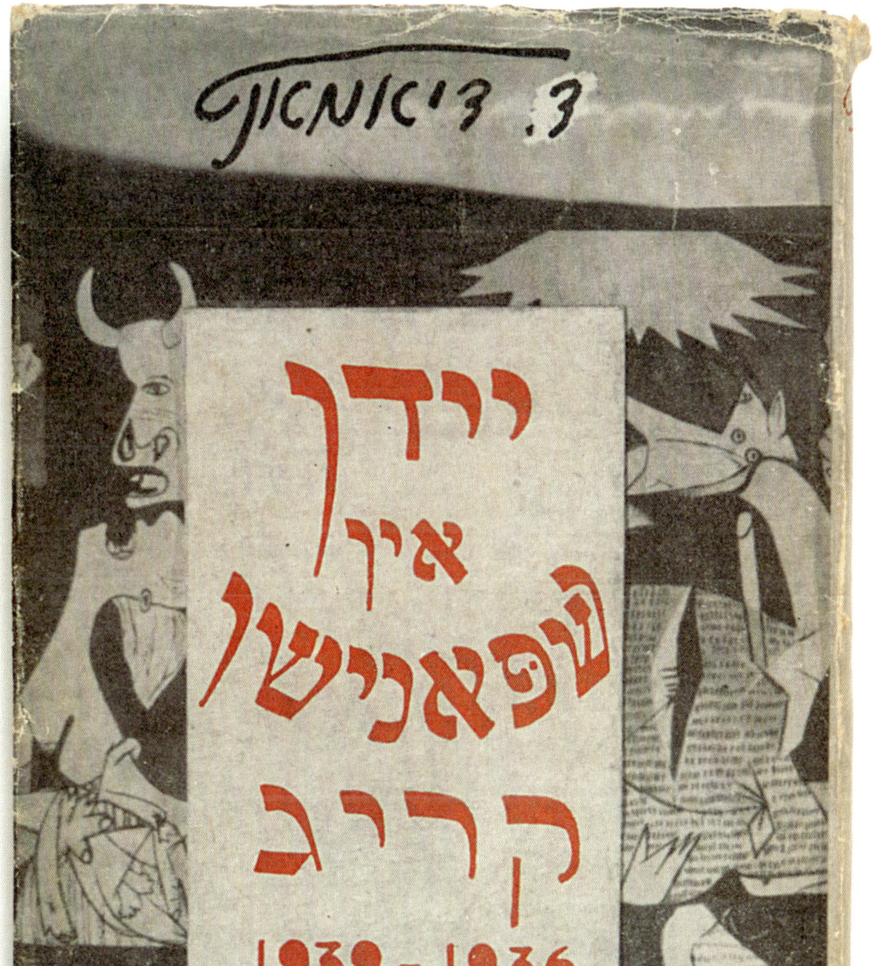
ז. דיאמאנט
יידן אין שפאנישן קריג
1936 - 1939

## DER KLEYNER PRINTS

(The Little Prince)

ANTOINE DE SAINT-EXUPÉRY (1900–1944)
TRANSLATED BY SHLOYME LERMAN (b. 1941),
NECKARSTEINACH, GERMANY, 2020

One of the best-selling books of all time, *The Little Prince* has been translated into hundreds of languages and adapted into films, plays, operas, and ballets. The Yiddish translation was first published in 2000 and places the Yiddish side by side with the original French.

ANTOINE DE SAINT-EXUPÉRY

# Der kleyner prints

## LE PETIT PRINCE

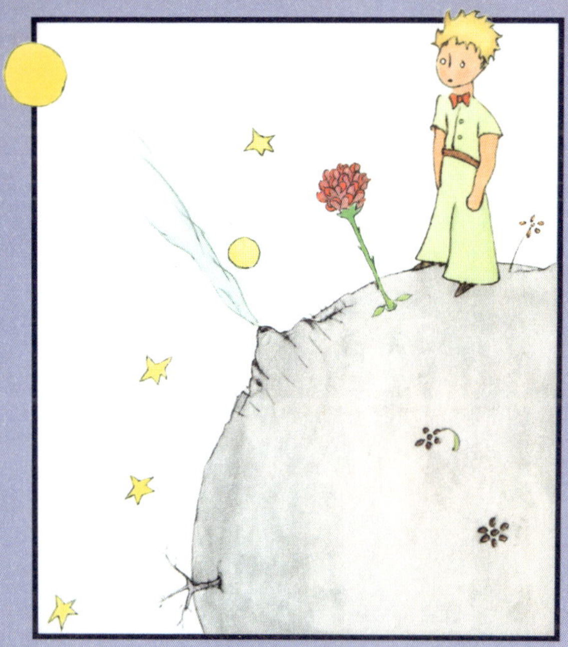

Yidish & Frantseyzish

Yiddish & Français

## Di opshtamung fun mentshen: un der opklayb beshaykhes tsu geshlekht, Band II

(The Descent of Man, and Selection in Relation to Sex, Volume 2)

CHARLES DARWIN (1809-1882)
TRANSLATED BY Y. A. MERISON (1866-1941), NEW YORK, 1921

Featuring a large portrait of Darwin on the dust jacket, this book is a translation of the pioneering biologist's work on human evolution and the theory of sexual selection. The translator, Y. A. Merison, was a radical activist and Columbia University–trained physician who also translated Karl Marx's *Das Kapital*.

טשאַרלז דאַרווין

די

# אָפּשטאַמונג פון מענשען

איבערזעצט פון דר. י. א. מעריסאָן

אין 3 בענד, אילוסטרירט

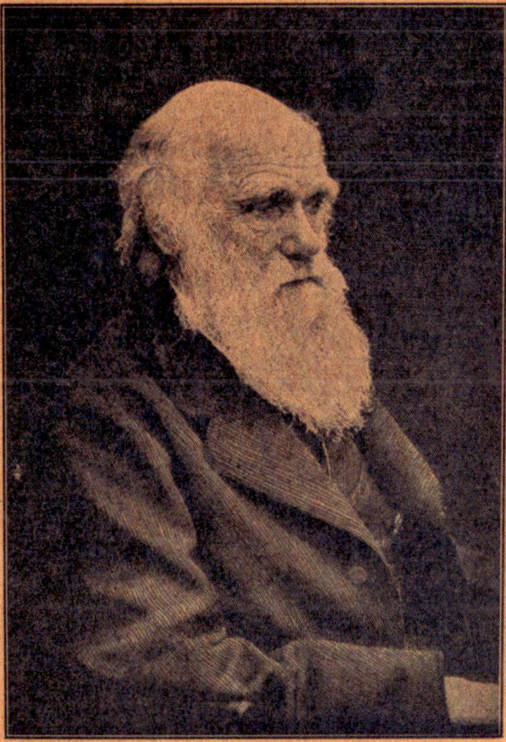

באנד II

## HERI POTER UN DER FILOSOFISHER SHTEYN

(Harry Potter and the Philosopher's Stone)

J. K. ROWLING (b. 1965)
TRANSLATED BY ARUN SCHAECHTER-VISWANATH (b. 1990),
LUND, SWEDEN, 2020

A native Yiddish speaker and member of a prominent Yiddishist family, American translator Arun Schaechter-Viswanath wanted the world of Harry Potter to be available for future generations of Yiddish-speaking children. Yiddishists of all ages responded enthusiastically to its publication by the Swedish publishing house Olniansky Tekst in 2020.

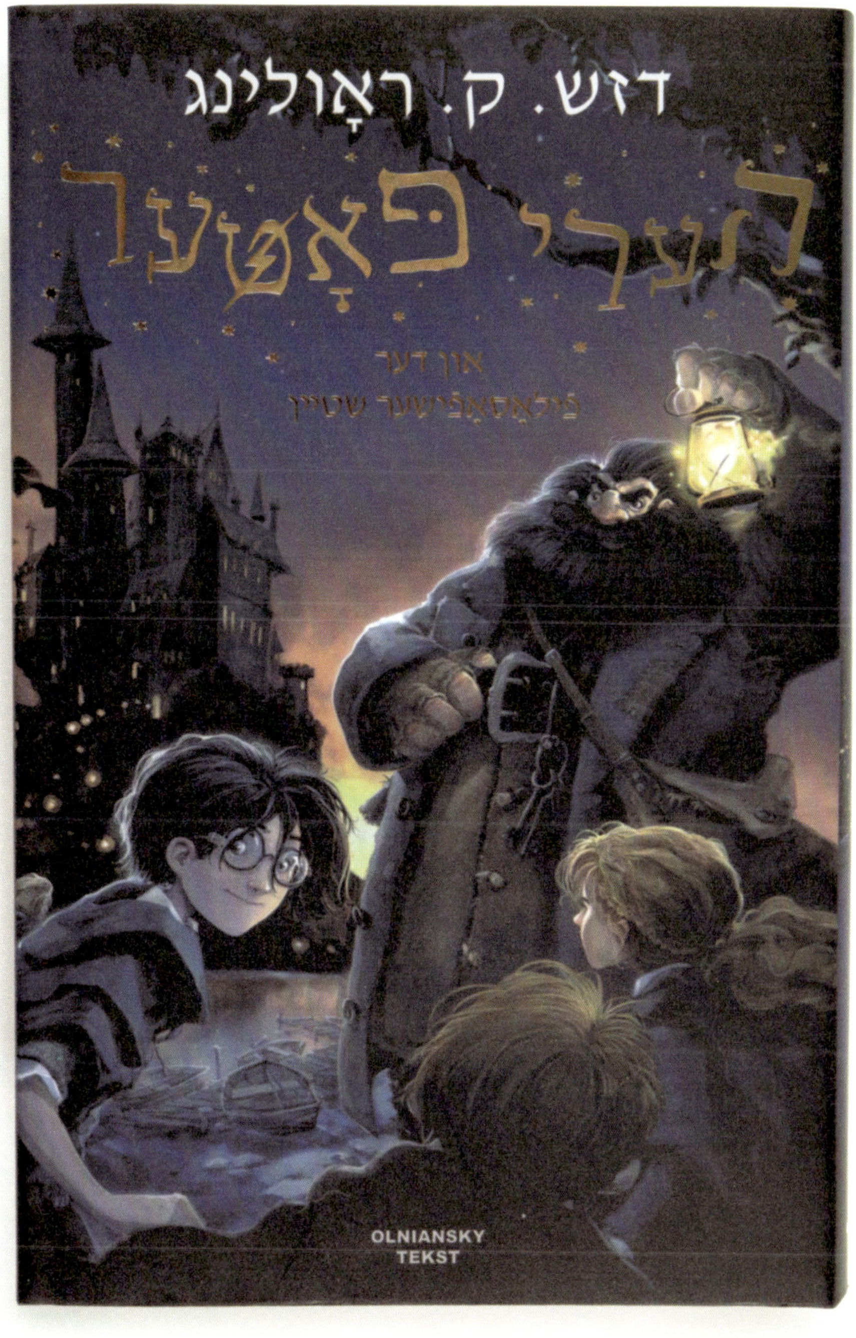

דזש. ק. ראָולינג
האַרי פּאָטער
און דער
פֿילאָסאָפֿישער שטיין
OLNIANSKY
TEKST

## PROLETARISHE YUGNT

(Proletarian Youth)

A. M. ORZYCER (1913-?), LONDON, 1943

A stark illustration of two young people leading a crowd in protest jumps out from the cover of this book of short stories. Orzycer was born in Poland and settled in London as a working tailor around 1932, during the high point of communist allegiance among the Jewish working class of London's East End.

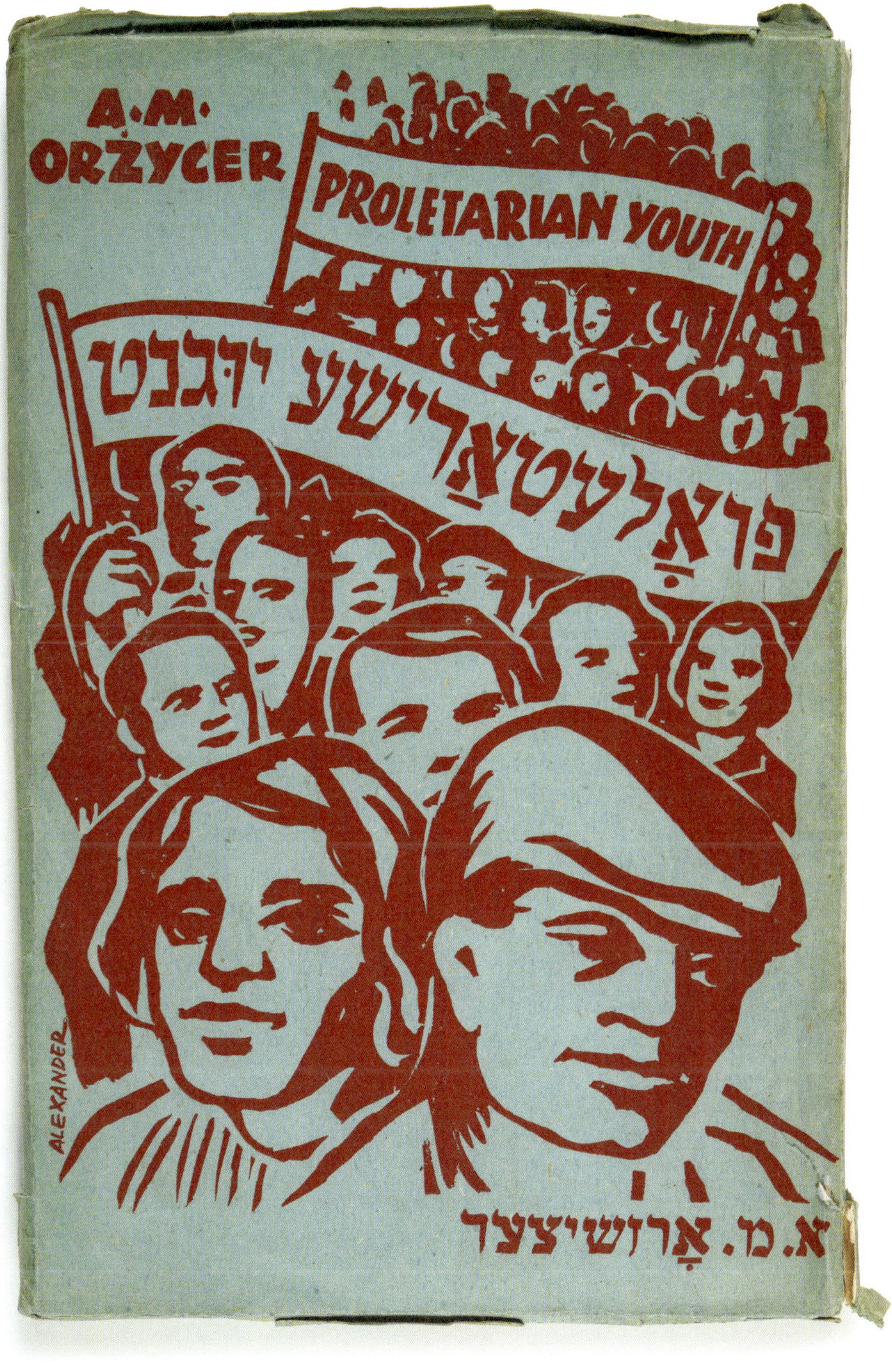
A.M.
ORŻYCER
PROLETARIAN YOUTH
פראָלעטאַרישע יוגנט
ALEXANDER
א. מ. אָרזשיצער

# DI SONETN FUN VILYAM SHEKSPIR

(William Shakespeare's Sonnets)

WILLIAM SHAKESPEARE (1564-1616)
TRANSLATED BY DR. AVROM AYSEN (1886-1965), NEW YORK, 1944

Translated into Yiddish by Lithuanian-born Avrom Aysen, this volume includes all 154 of Shakespeare's sonnets. Over the course of his career, Aysen also translated Lord Byron, Henry Wadsworth Longfellow, and Walt Whitman into Yiddish.

# די סאָנעטן

## פון

# וו. שעקספּיר

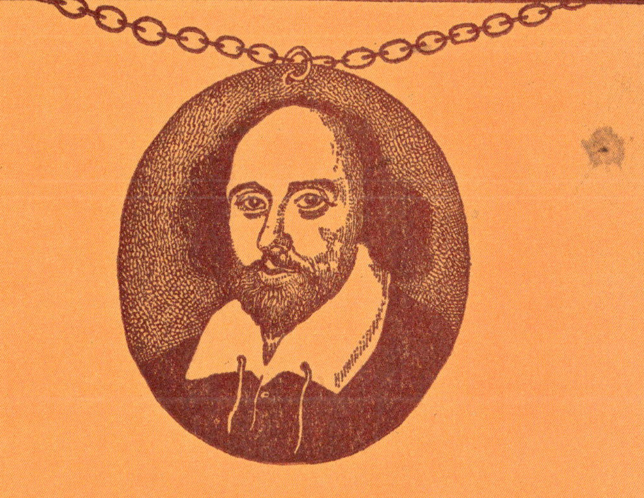

אידיש פון

## דר. א. אייסען

ש.ר.

# KALEVALA

## (Land of Heroes)

ELIAS LÖNNROT (1802-1884),
TRANSLATED BY HERSH ROZENFELD (1884-1960), NEW YORK, 1954

Poet and translator Hersh Rozenfeld trained as a chemist and worked in the laundry business and auto industry before producing his translation of *Kalevala*, the national folk epic of Finland. In Finnish, *Kalevala* means "land of heroes," and the epic tale has been translated into over twenty languages.

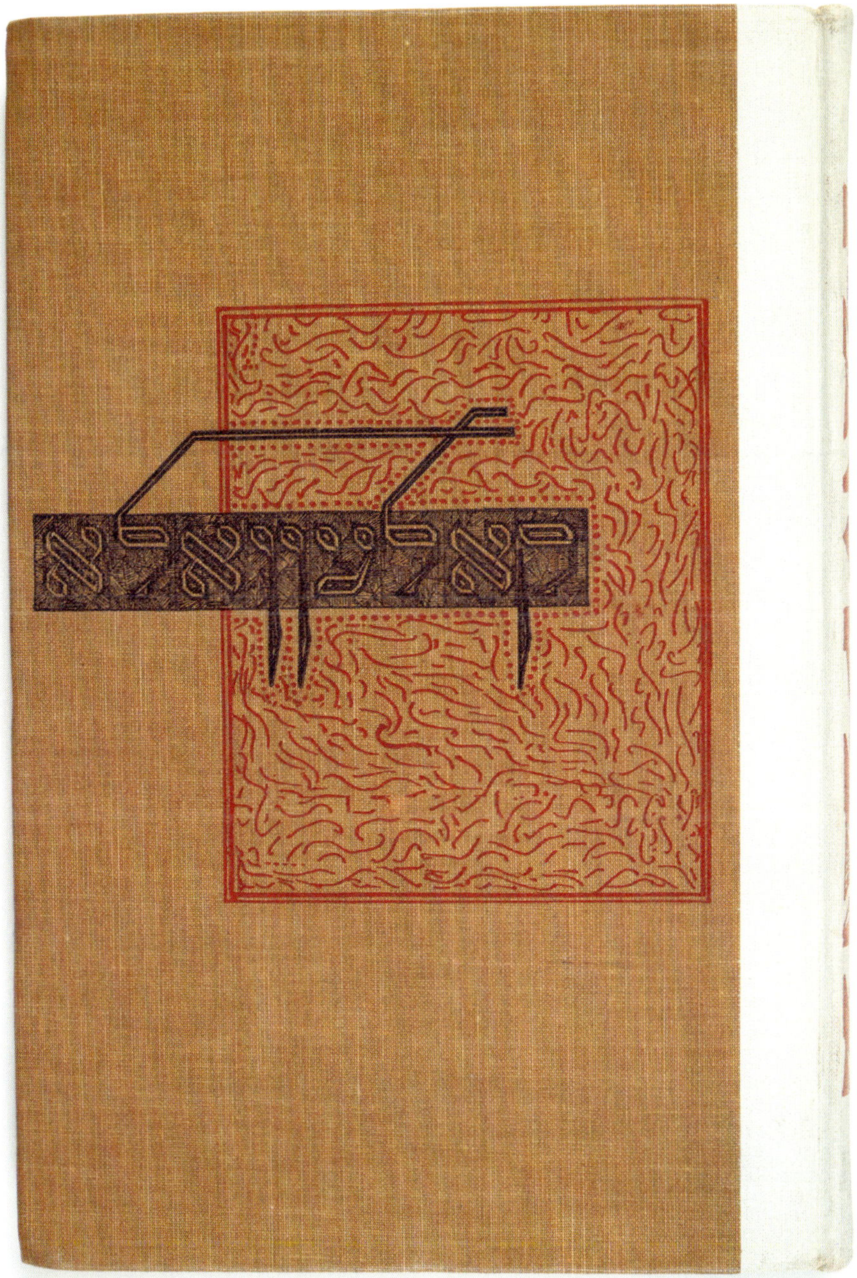

# DOS TOGBUKH FUN ANA FRANK

(The Diary of Anne Frank)

ANNE FRANK (1929-1945)
TRANSLATED BY ESTHER HALPERN (?-?), BUENOS AIRES, 1958

One of three different Yiddish translations of the international best seller, this Buenos Aires edition appeared simultaneously with one in Tel Aviv and a few years before another in Bucharest. *The Diary of Anne Frank* has been translated into approximately seventy languages worldwide.

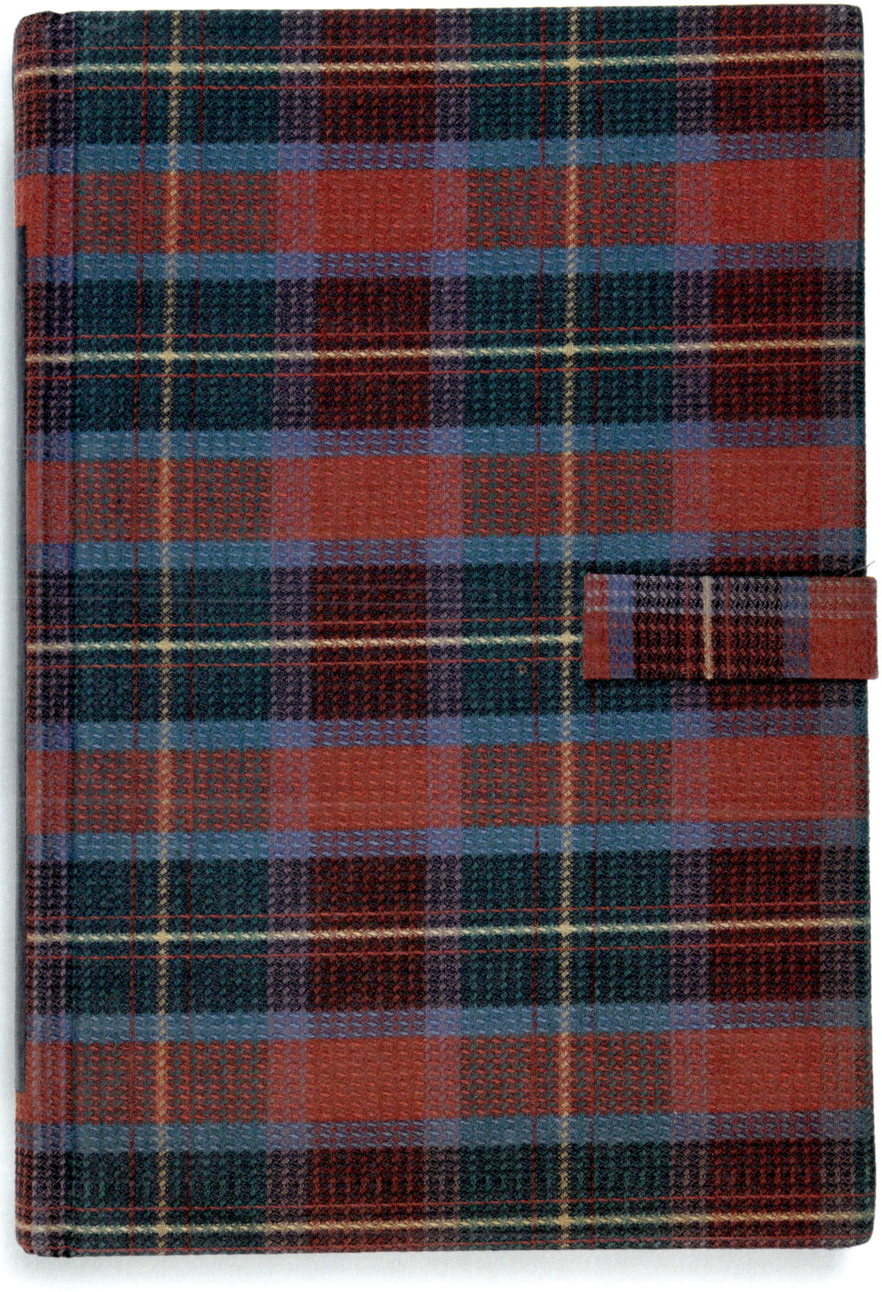

## IN DI OREMS FUN TOYT

(In the Arms of Death)

MORDKHE SARNA (1917-?), PARIS, 1946

This early attempt to commemorate the Holocaust through Yiddish literature features several black and white illustrations accompanying eerie stories of physical and mental anguish. The stark cover image captures both the aggressor—a knife-wielding skeleton wearing a Nazi helmet—and the defiance shown by the many Jews who resisted the Nazis.

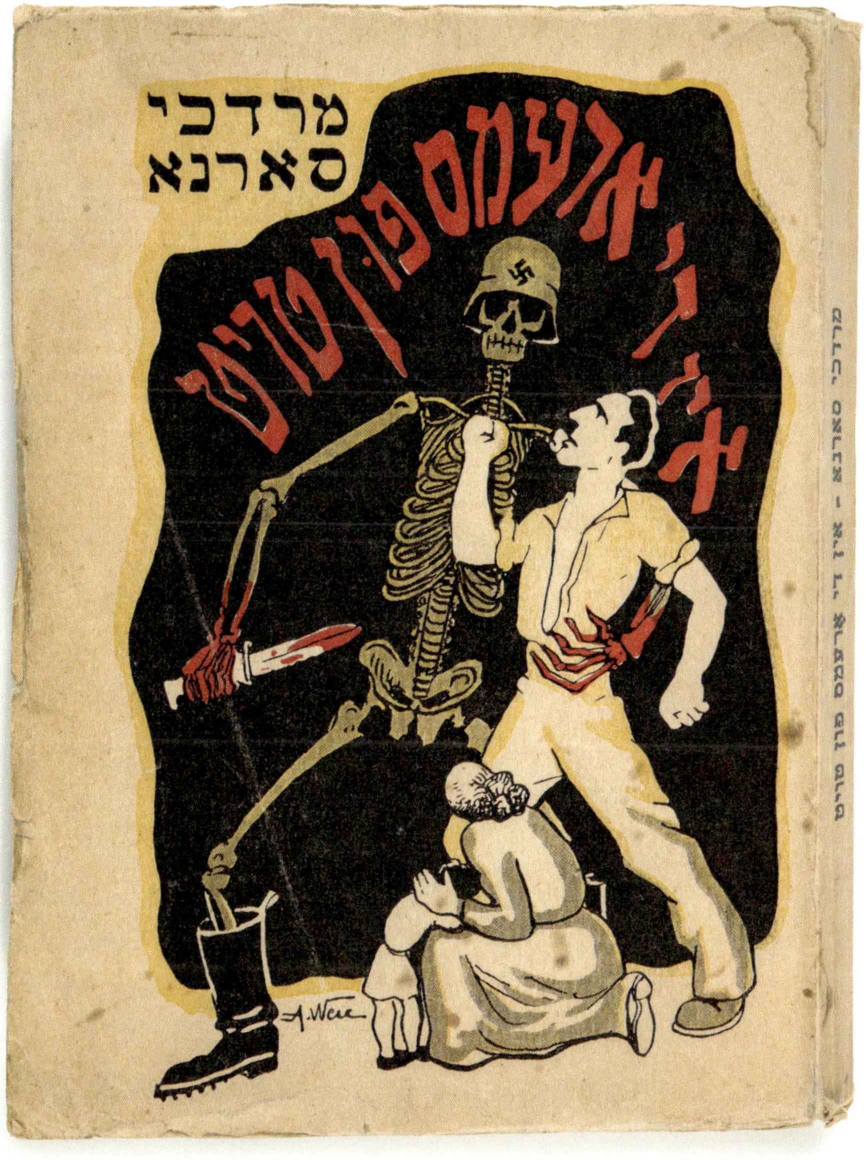
מרדכי
סארנא

## HITLERS GEBURT

(Hitler's Birth)

SHOLEM ASCH (1880-1957), NEW YORK, 1944

With its illustration of a villainous frog on a striking green and red cover, this novella by Sholem Asch crafts an origin story for Hitler. Published in New York in 1944 by the left-wing newspaper and publisher *Morgn-frayhayt (Morning Freedom)*, *Hitlers geburt* fuses truth and legend to spin a tale based in Hitler's home city of Braunau, on the border of Austria and Germany.

# היטלערס געבורט

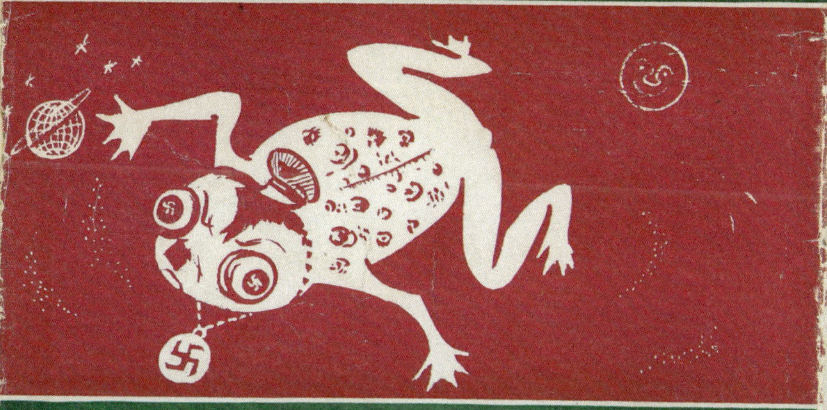

פון שלום אש

## AFN VEG TSUM ZIG: TIPN FUN YIDISHE PARTIZANER

(On the Road to Victory: Portraits of Jewish Partisans)

MOYSHE GILDENMAN (1898-1957), PARIS, 1949

In 1942 Moyshe Gildenman escaped the Korets Ghetto with his son and became a partisan commander, leading a fighting group of over 1,400 people. Writing under the Russian partisan name Dyadya Misha (Uncle Misha), Gildenman dedicates this book to "My unforgettable comrades in the struggle, who died for the honor of the Jewish people and whose graves are scattered across the forests of Ukraine and Belarus."

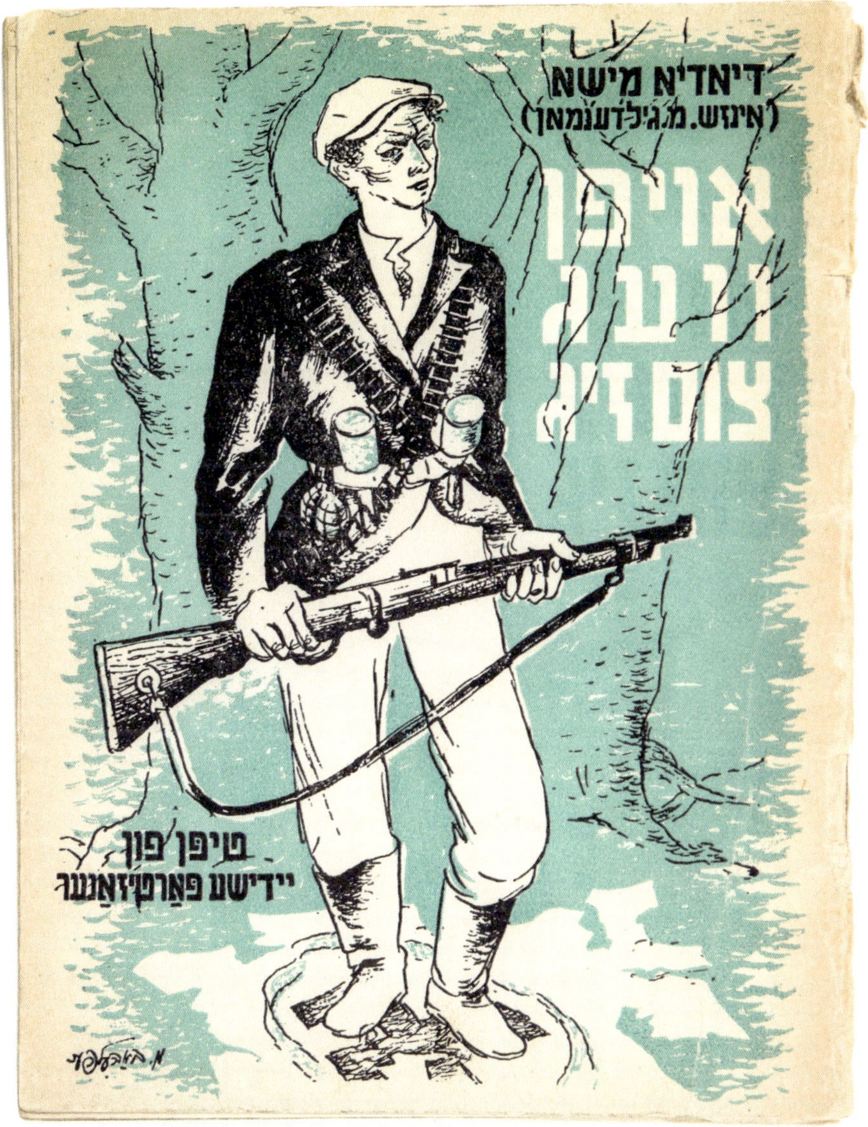
דיאדיא מישא
(אינזש. מ. גילדענמאן)
אויפן וועג צום זיג
טיפן פון
יידישע פארטיזאנער

## VILNER GETO

(Vilna Ghetto)

AVROM SUTZKEVER (1913-2010), PARIS, 1946

This book chronicles the destruction of Vilna, the "Jerusalem of Lithuania." During the war, poet Avrom Sutzkever was assigned by the Nazis to a group tasked with dismantling the YIVO (Yiddish Scientific Institute) archives and shipping the contents to Germany. Instead Sutzkever and his comrades in the "Paper Brigade" smuggled out and saved hundreds of rare books and artifacts.

א. סוצקעווער

# ווילנער געטאָ

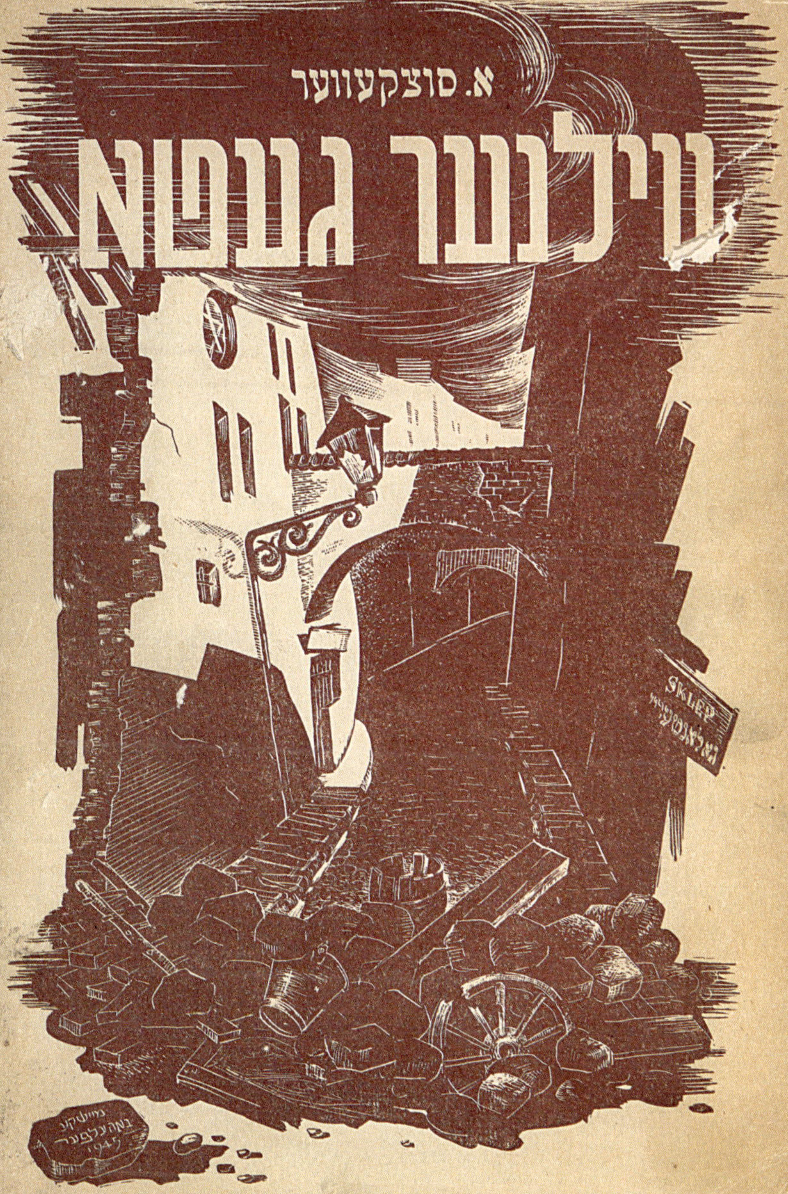

## “UMLEGALE” YIDN SHPALTN YAMEN
### (“Illegal” Jews Part the Seas)

SHMUEL IZBAN (1905-1995), BUENOS AIRES, 1948

A packed boat fighting through choppy seas illustrates the tale within. This book tells the story of refugees escaping Europe as part of Aliya Bet, the second wave of Jewish immigrants to Mandatory Palestine. Shmuel Izban, a lifelong newspaperman, joined one of these dangerous voyages in 1947 on assignment for the New York Yiddish daily *Der morgn zhurnal* (*The Morning Journal*).

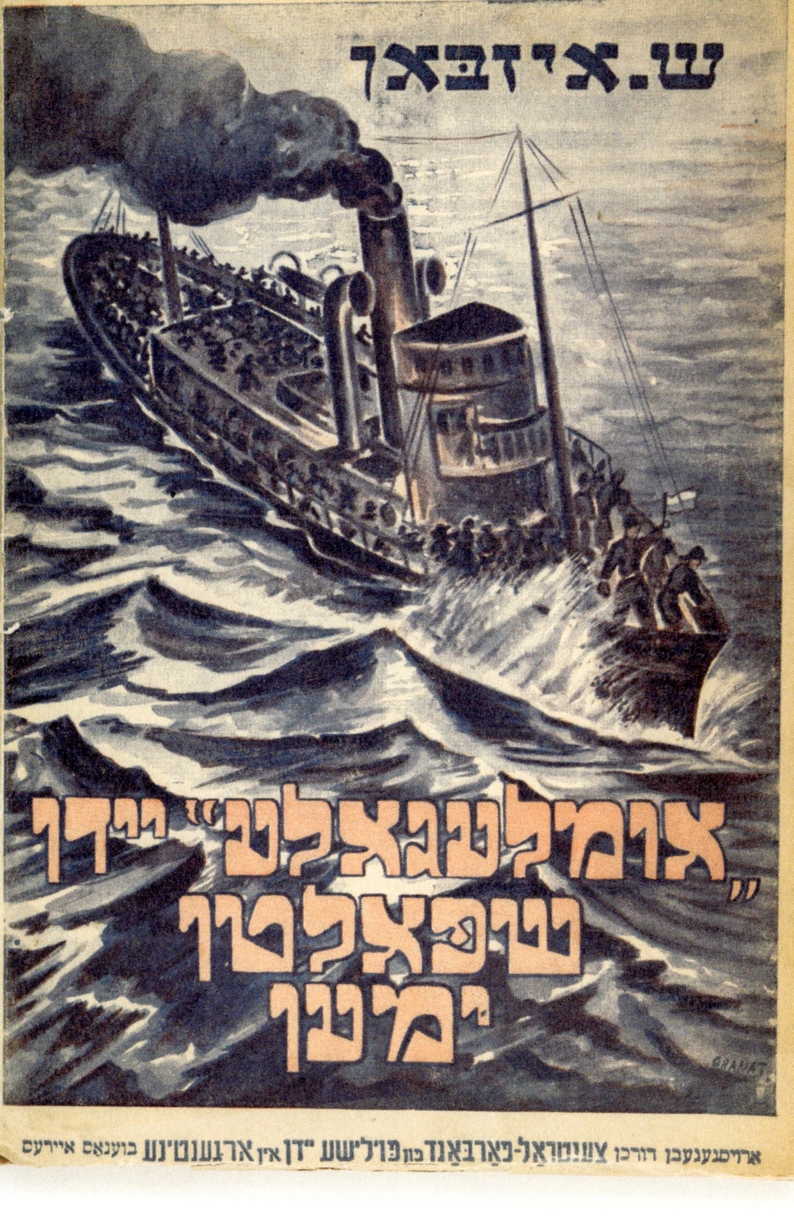


אַרויסגעגעבן דורכן צענטראַל-פֿאַרבאַנד פֿון פּוילישע ײדן אין אַרגענטינע בוענאָס איירעס

## ERSHTER KONGRES FARN ARBETNDN ERETS-YISROEL

(First Congress of the Workers of the Land of Israel)

*VELT-LIGE FARN ARBETNDN ERETS-YISROEL* (*INTERNATIONAL LEAGUE OF WORKERS OF THE LAND OF ISRAEL*), WARSAW, 1931

The conference of the International League of Workers of the Land of Israel was held in Berlin from September 27 to October 1, 1930, though this book was published in Warsaw. The cover displays a map of Palestine behind a person waving a red flag, encapsulating the excitement about the new organization of workers in Mandatory Palestine, as well as the strength of left-wing groups within the Zionist movement.

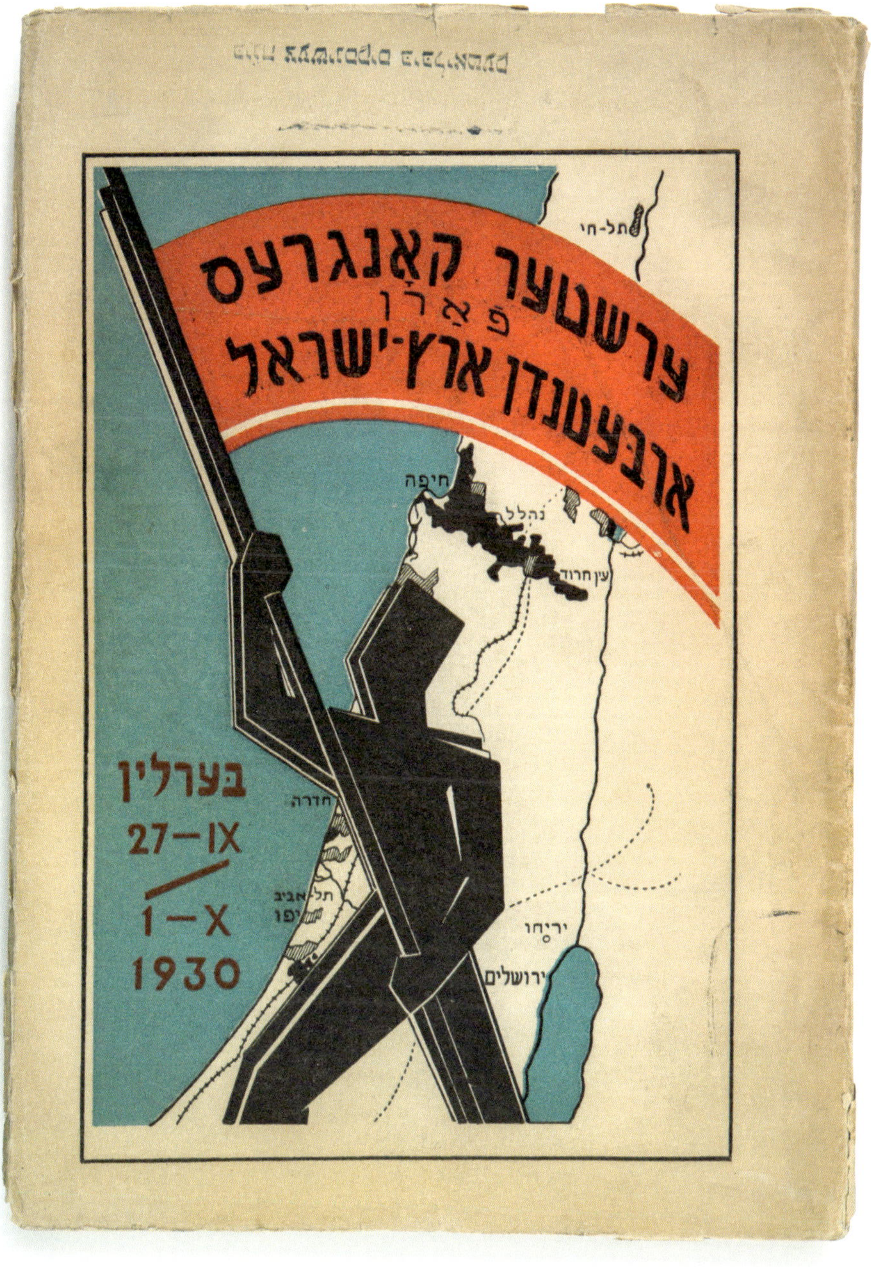
ערשטער קאָנגרעס
פֿאַרן
ארבעטנדן ארץ-ישראל
בערלין
27—IX
1—X
1930
תל-חי
חיפה
נהלל
עין חרוד
חדרה
תל-אביב
יפו
יריחו
ירושלים

## Erets Yisroel: in Fargangenhayt un Gegenvart

(The Land of Israel: Past and Present)

DAVID BEN-GURION (1886-1973) AND YITZHAK BEN-ZVI (1884-1963), NEW YORK, 1918

Published by the Marxist-Zionist Poale Zion movement, this book was meant to acquaint Yiddish readers with the history and geography of Palestine. The book was co-authored by David Ben-Gurion, who later became the first prime minister of Israel, and Yitzhak Ben-Zvi, president of Israel from 1952 to 1963.

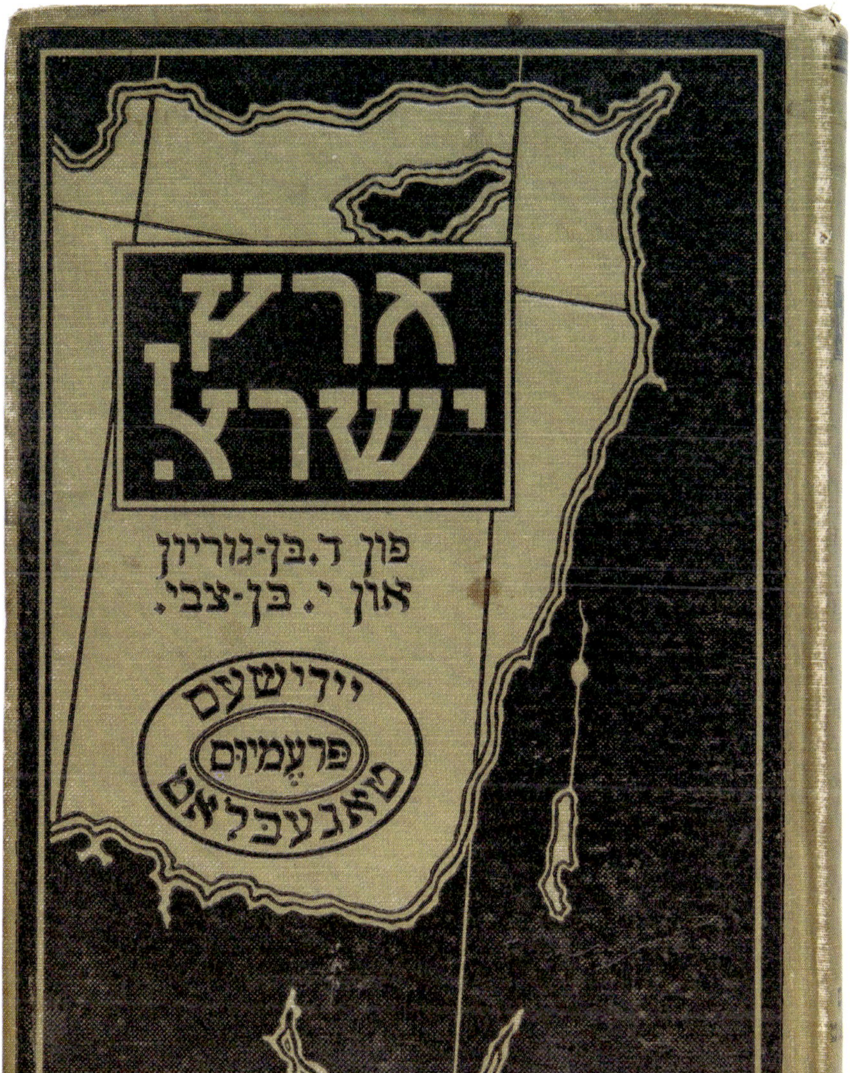
ארץ ישראל
פון ד. בן-גוריון
און י. בן-צבי.
יידישעס
פרעמיום
פאגעבלאם

## ARABISH-IDISHER LEHRER: VEG VAYZER FAR DI IDISHE LEGYONERN IN TSIYON

(Arabic-Yiddish Teacher: Guidebook for Jewish Legionnaires in Zion)

GEORGE SELIKOVITCH (1863-1926), NEW YORK, 1918

Intended for Yiddish-speaking soldiers fighting with the British in Palestine, this handbook promises that the reader will "acquire in a month the spoken Arabic of Palestine and Egypt." Its author, Getsl Zelikovitsh (George Selikovitch), was an Arabic-English interpreter for the British army in Sudan, a professor of Egyptology, and a hugely prolific writer in Hebrew, Yiddish, Arabic, French, and English.

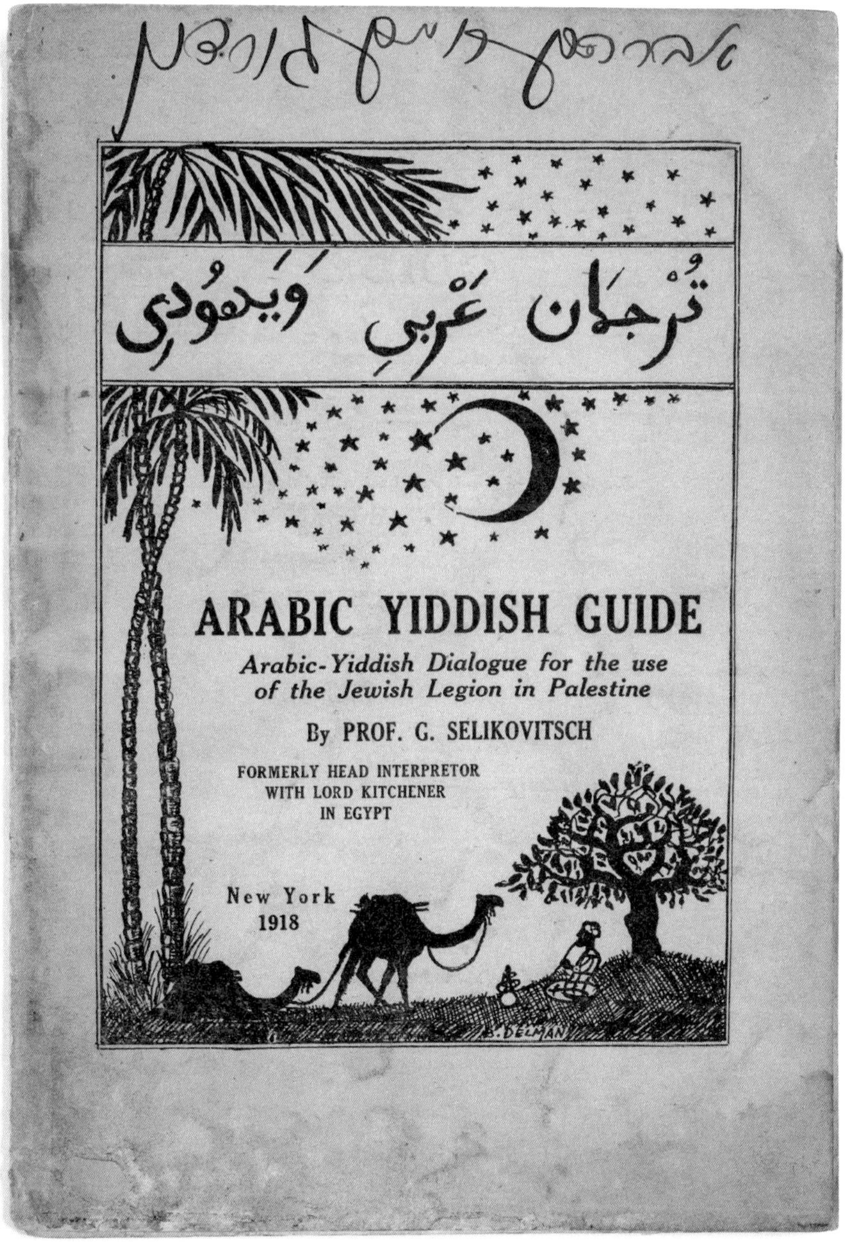
ترجمان عربي ويهودي
ARABIC YIDDISH GUIDE
Arabic-Yiddish Dialogue for the use of the Jewish Legion in Palestine
By PROF. G. SELIKOVITSCH
FORMERLY HEAD INTERPRETOR WITH LORD KITCHENER IN EGYPT
New York
1918
B. DELMAN

## SHEKHEREZADES NEKHT

(Scheherazade's Nights / The Thousand and One Nights)

UNKNOWN TRANSLATOR, WARSAW, 1923

An elegantly dressed camel and rider adorn the cover of this Yiddish translation of *The Thousand and One Nights*. The Yiddish title differs from the standard English version in emphasizing the narrator of the stories, Scheherazade, who tells the tales to her husband, the Persian king Shahryar, to forestall her execution.

165

# שעהערעזאַדעס
# נעכט

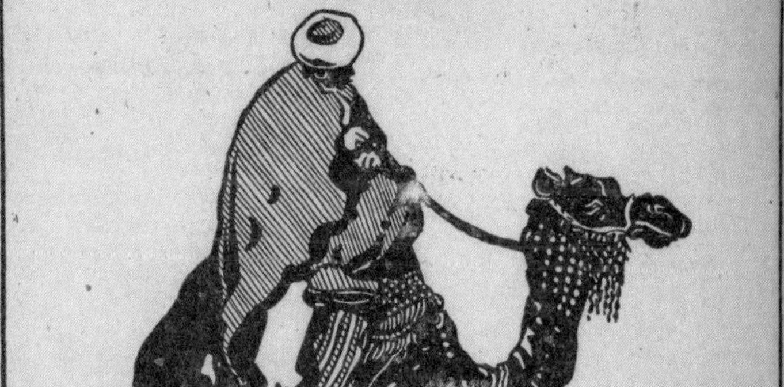

## MOHAMED: GRINDER FUN MOHAMEDIZMUS

(Mohammed: Founder of Mohammedanism)

PHILIP KRANTZ (1858-1922), NEW YORK, 1907

Written by radical activist, journalist, and popular-science author Philip Krantz, this pamphlet introduces readers to the life of Mohammed and the establishment of Islam. Krantz published many such books to educate the Yiddish-speaking masses, including biographies of figures ranging from Simon bar Kokhba to Aristotle.

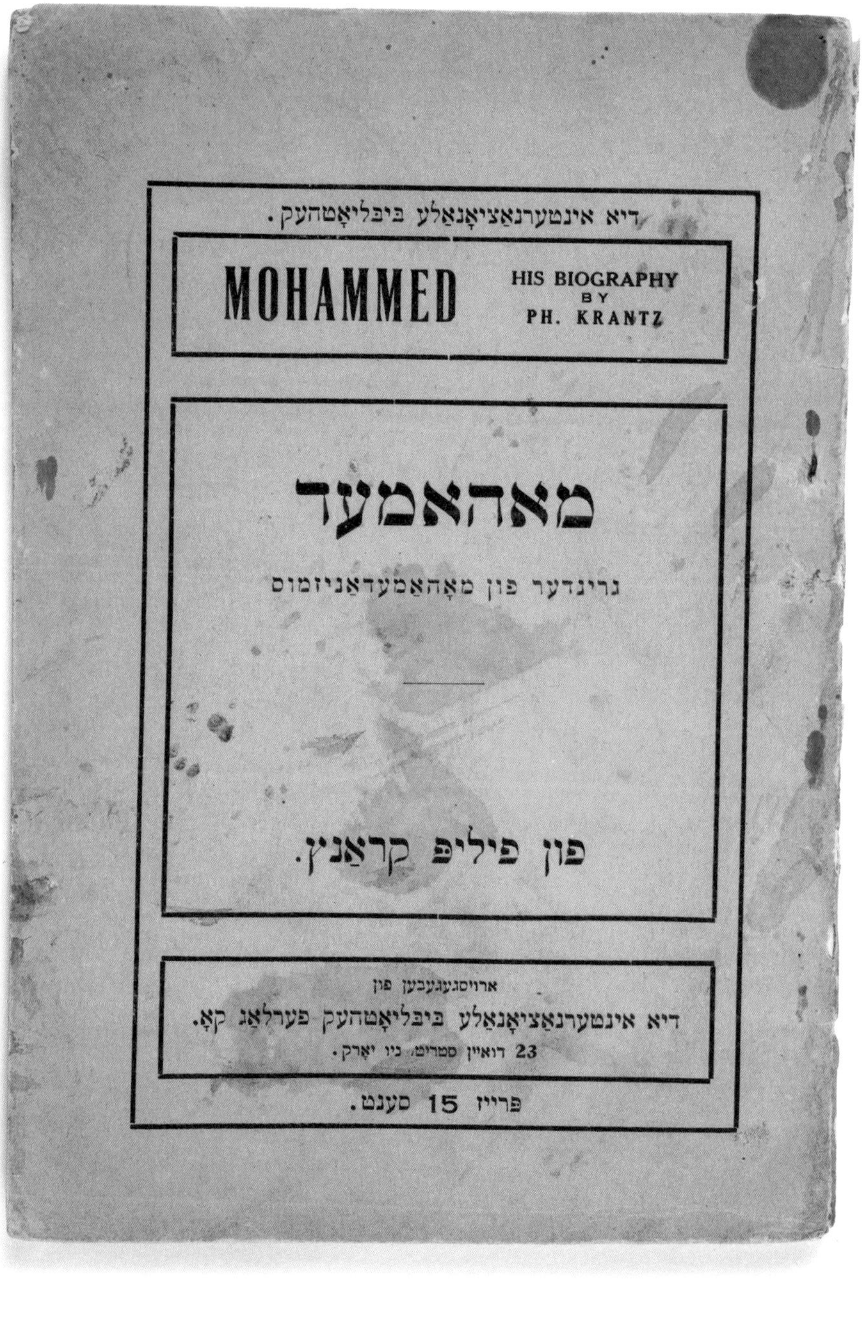
די אינטערנאַציאָנאַלע ביבליאָטהעק.
MOHAMMED
HIS BIOGRAPHY
BY
PH. KRANTZ
מאהאמעד
גרינדער פון מאָהאַמעדאַניזמוס
פון פיליפ קראַנץ.
ארויסגעגעבען פון
די אינטערנאַציאָנאַלע ביבליאָטהעק פערלאַג קאָ.
23 דואיין סטריט, ניו יאָרק.
פרייז 15 סענט.

## Durkh umbakante lender

(Through Unknown Lands)

KHAYIM SHOSHKES (1891-1964), RIO DE JANEIRO, 1954

Khayim Shoshkes was a world traveler and a worker for aid organizations such as HIAS, the Hebrew Immigrant Aid Society. This volume, with the multicultural collage on its cover, describes Jewish communities ranging from Holocaust refugees in Singapore to the last remaining Jews of Beirut to the Beta Israel people in the mountains of Ethiopia.

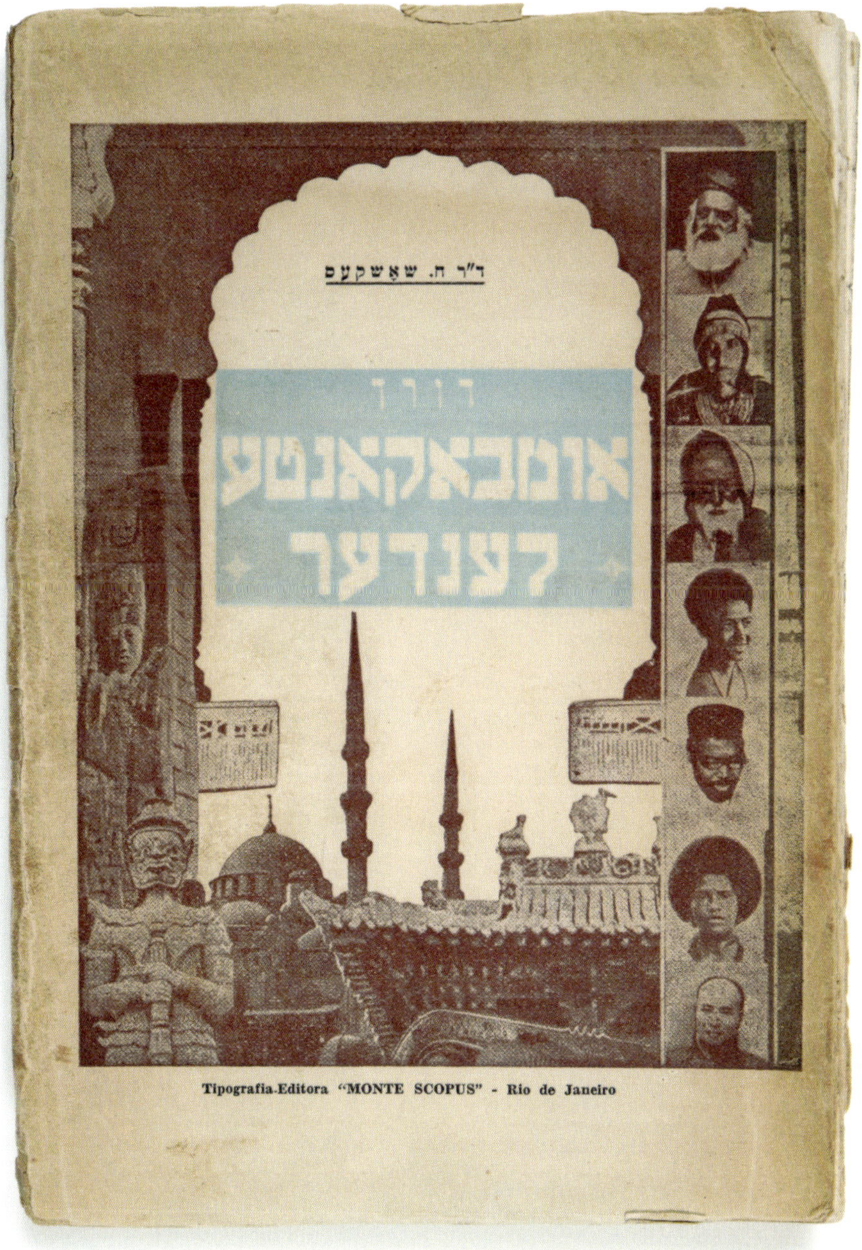
ד״ר ח. שאָשקעס
דורך
אומבאַקאַנטע
לענדער
Tipografia-Editora "MONTE SCOPUS" - Rio de Janeiro

# KAVKAZER LIBE: OPERETE IN 3 AKTN

## (Love in the Caucasus: Operetta in 3 Acts)

A. FRAYMAN (YISROEL ROSENBERG) (1895-1963), WARSAW, 1926

The photographs on the cover are the only images remaining of this Yiddish operetta production, but set descriptions imply a feast for the senses, with a backdrop of forests and waterfalls behind a choir and dancers. The music was composed by Peretz Sandler, who also worked on productions such as *Mendel in Japan*, *Romani Love*, *The Jew in Morocco*, and *Chaste Shoshana*.

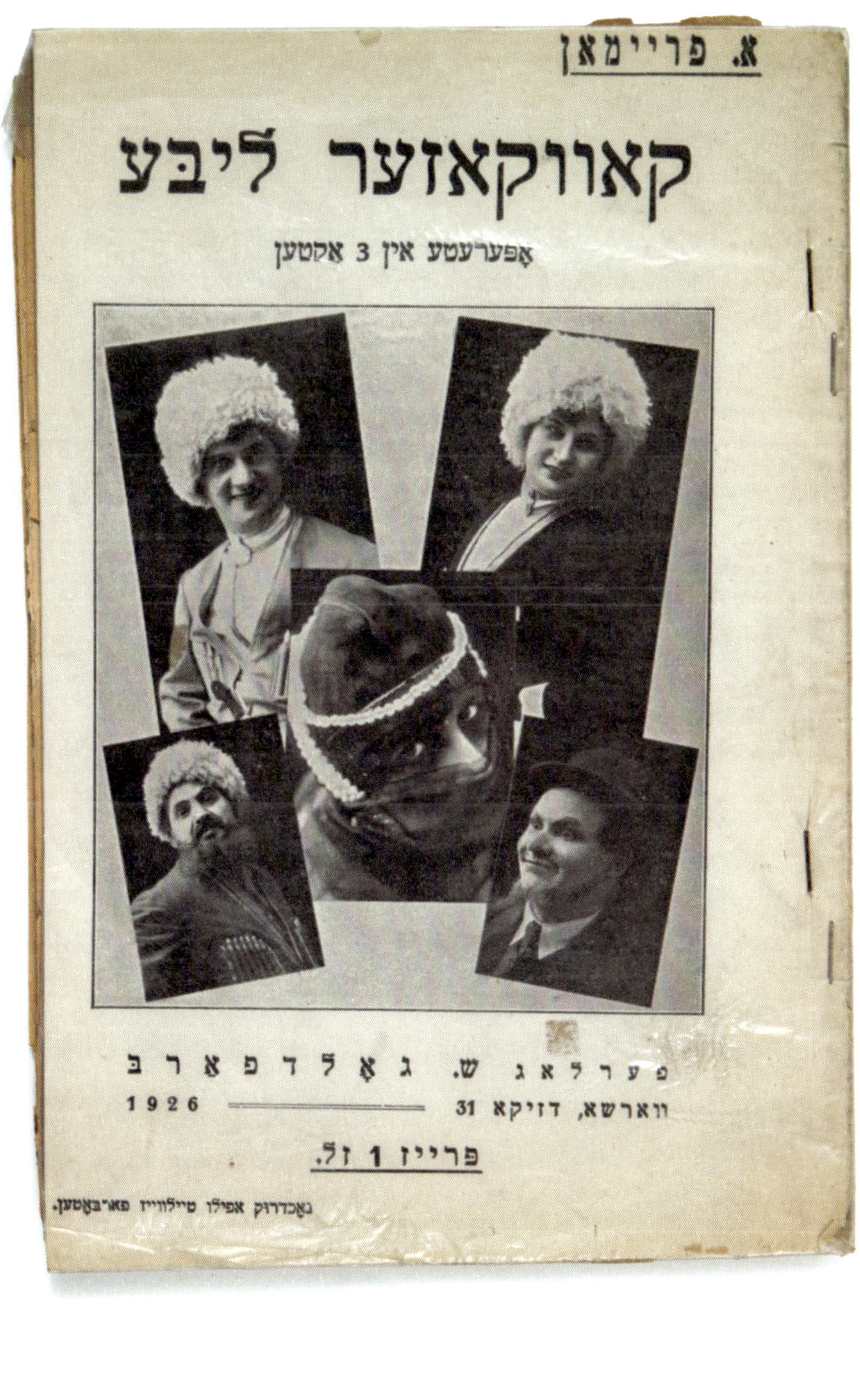
א. פריימאן
קאווקאזער ליבּע
אָפּערעטע אין 3 אַקטען
פערלאג ש. גאָלדפארב
ווארשא, דזיקא 31
1926
פרייז 1 זל.
נאַכדרוק אפילו טיילווייז פאַרבאָטן.

# RUBAYAT

(Rubaiyat)

OMAR KHAYAM (1048-1131)
TRANSLATED BY DR. A. AYSEN (1886-1965), NEW YORK, 1926

The *Rubaiyat of Omar Khayam* was the 1859 title given by English poet Edward FitzGerald to his translation of Persian astronomer Omar Khayam. Though the authenticity of Khayam's poetry has been debated, FitzGerald's translation popularized the text in the English-speaking world. Avrom Aysen, known for his translation of Shakespeare's sonnets, rendered it into Yiddish in 1926, opening up Persian poetry to the Yiddish-speaking world.

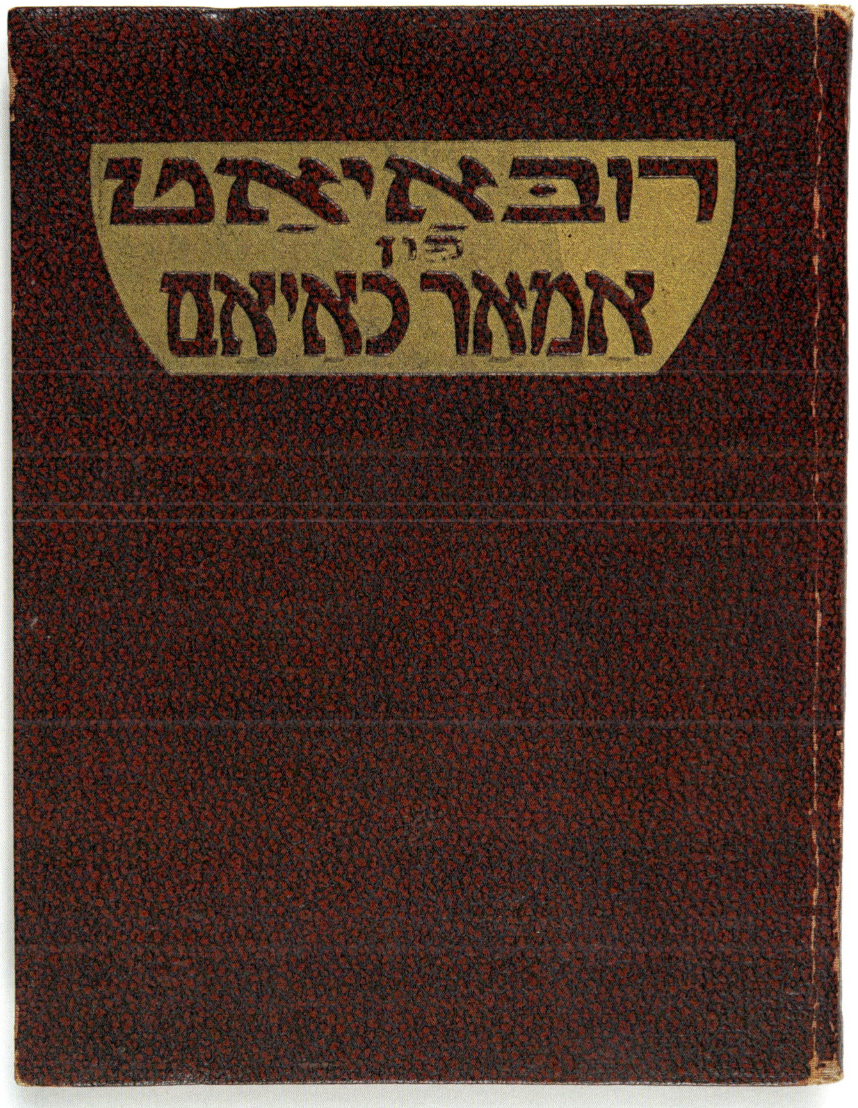
רובאיאט
פון
אמאר כאיאם

## DOS BUKH FUN DZSHONGL

(The Jungle Book)

RUDYARD KIPLING (1865-1936)
TRANSLATED BY LAMED SHAPIRO (1878-1948), VILNA, 1913

This 1913 translation of Kipling's 1894 children's classic was one of many by Ukrainian-born Yiddish writer Lamed Shapiro, alongside works by Victor Hugo, Sir Walter Scott, and Charles Dickens. The collection of stories centers around the adventures of a boy named Mowgli, who is being raised by wolves in an Indian forest.

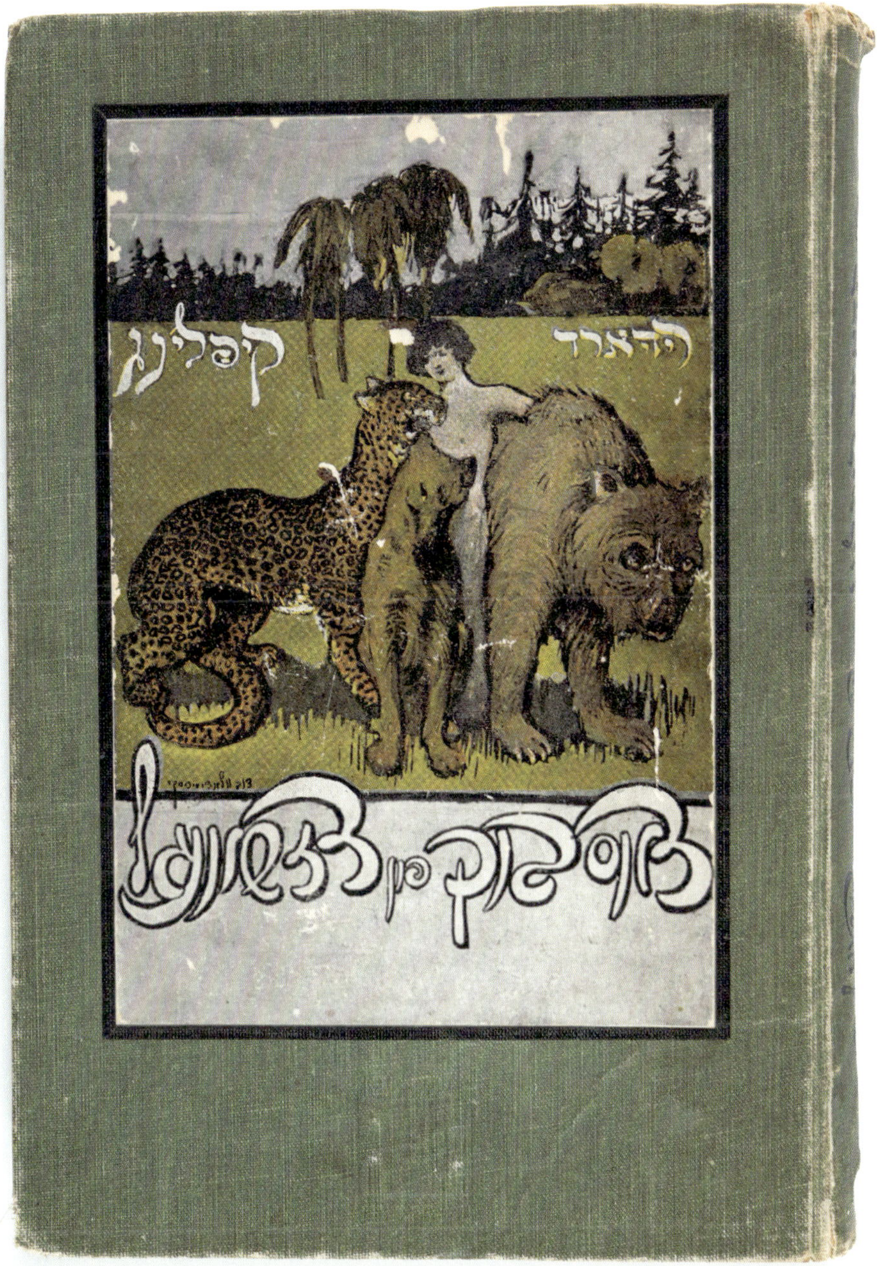

רודיארד קיפלינג
דאס בוך פון דזשונגל

## UZBEKISTAN, TIPN UN BILDER

(Uzbekistan: Characters and Images)

MEYLEKH TSHEMNI (1910-?), MUNICH, 1949

Polish-born author Meylekh Tshemni conveys the warmth of Central Asia's climate in this book, as does the cover illustration of a palm tree. Tshemni was born and raised in Warsaw but fled to Bialystok at the beginning of World War II and subsequently lived in Tashkent and Samarkand from 1941 to 1945. He published this book himself upon returning to Warsaw in 1949.

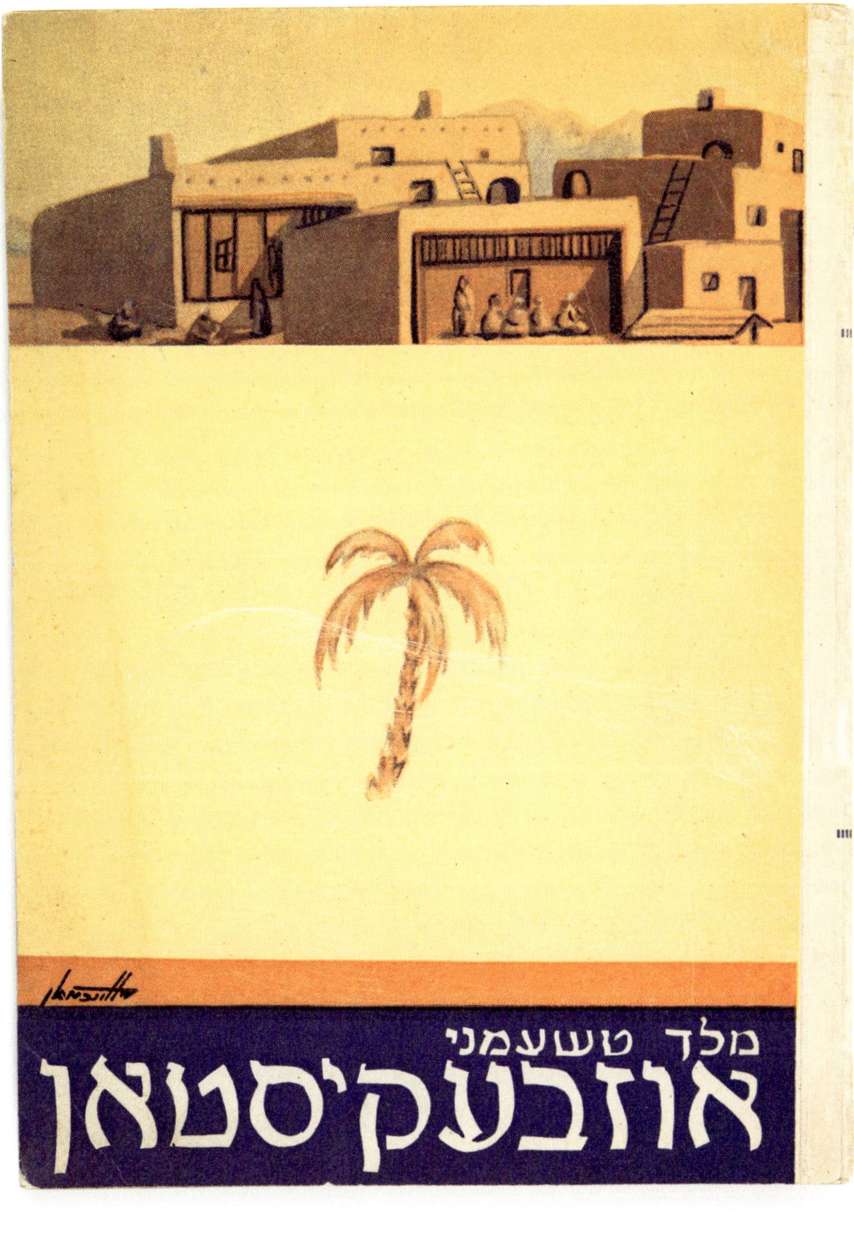
מלך טשעמני
אוזבעקיסטאן

## LIDER FUN TFISE UN LAGER
(Poems from Prison and Camp)

SHMUEL HALKIN (1897-1960), TEL AVIV, 1988

Russian Jewish poet Shmuel Halkin stares back at us from the cover of this book, his face pasted onto a prisoner's uniform, with the stylized bars of a prison cell behind him. A member of the Jewish Anti-Fascist Committee during World War II, Halkin was arrested in 1950 and wrote these poems while imprisoned in the Gulag. Unlike many others, he was spared execution and was released in 1955.

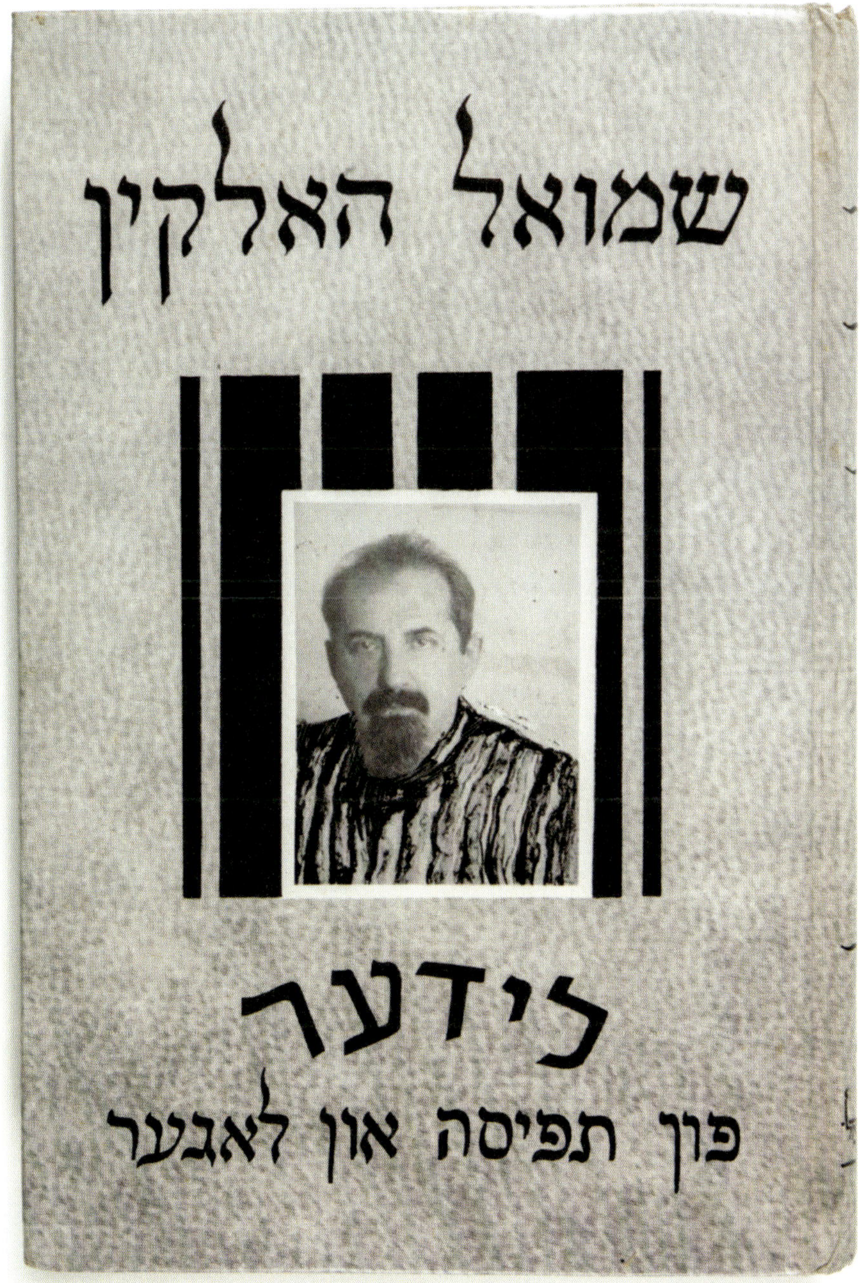
שמואל האלקין
לידער
פון תפיסה און לאגער

# Birobidzhan: Shilderungen fun a Rayze in Yuli-Oygust 1934

(Birobidzhan: Descriptions of a Trip in July–August 1934)

OSHER PERELMAN (1895-?), WARSAW, 1934

Perelman, a Polish Yiddish journalist, gives a glowing account of a trip to Birobidzhan, the Jewish autonomous (self-governing) region in the Soviet far east. A passionate believer in Soviet Communism, Perelman moved to Moscow in 1935, was arrested in 1937, accused of "Jewish nationalism," and spent eighteen years in a Soviet labor camp. Freed in 1955, he emerged sick and broken in spirit.

א. פערעלמאַן

# ביראָבידזשאַן

שילדערונגען פון א רייזע
אין יולי–אויגוסט 1934.

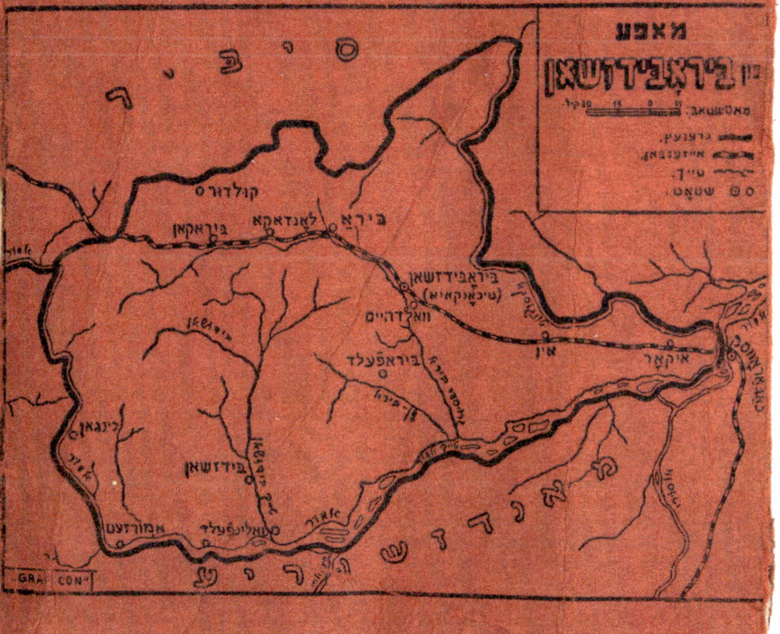

## KHINE
(China)

LEIZER BAUMGARTEN (1902-?), VILNA, 1940

Before writing this book, Baumgarten traveled to China to write a series of articles for *Haynt* (*Today*), a Yiddish daily based in Warsaw. He illustrated this history of the Republic of China with photos from his journey, and it was likely one of the last Yiddish books published in Vilna before the Holocaust. The cover uses a photo taken on one of his trips, with the title written on the woman's arm.

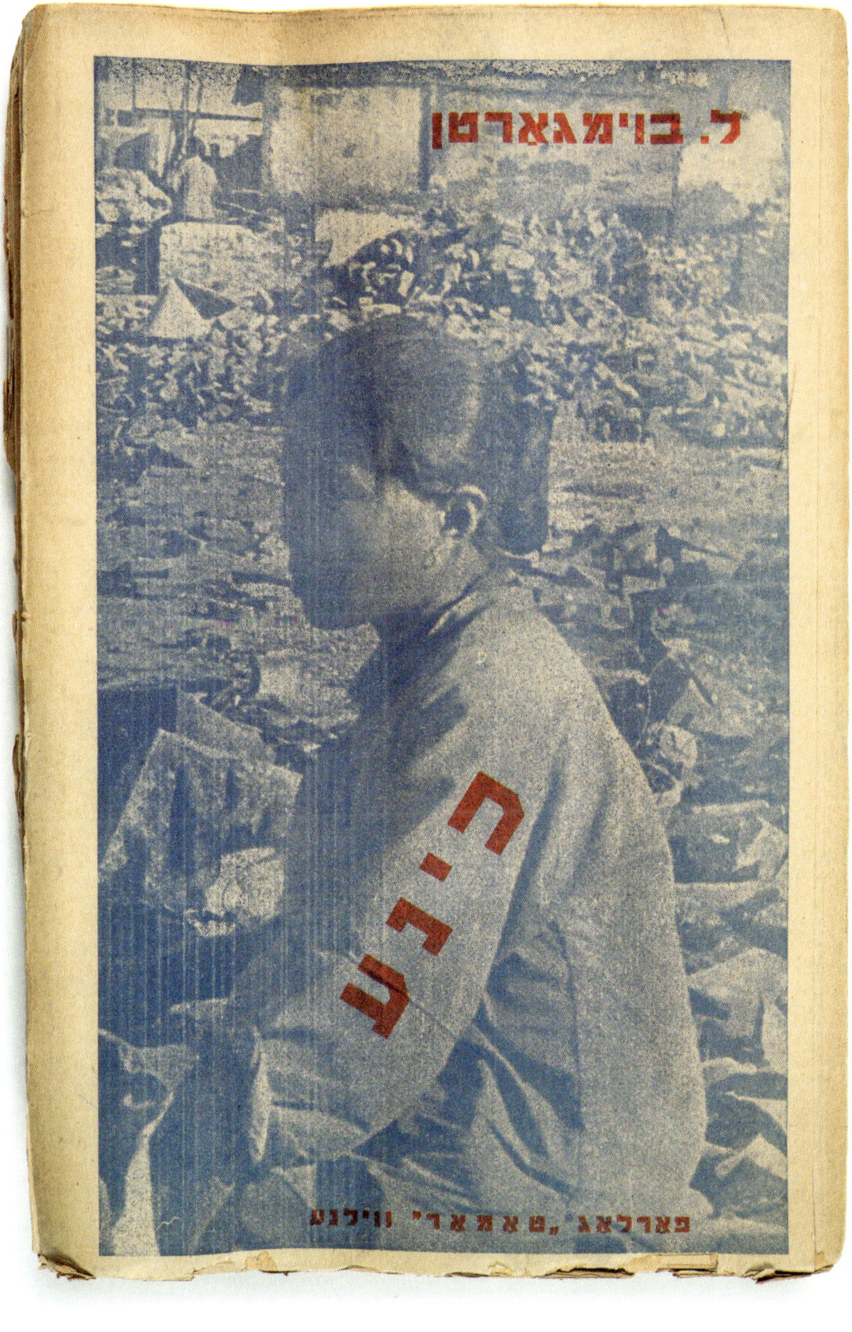
ל. בוימגארטן
חינע
פארלאג „טאמאר" ווילנע

## YAPANISHE MAYSELEKH

(Japanese Tales)

TRANSLATED BY M. RAKOVSKI (1890-1982)
ABRIDGED BY P. KAPLAN (1870-1943)

This children's book was translated from Japanese in 1921 by the prolific multilingual Mark Rakovski, a Russian-born writer who rendered dozens of classics of world literature into Yiddish.

# יאפאנישע מעשהלאך

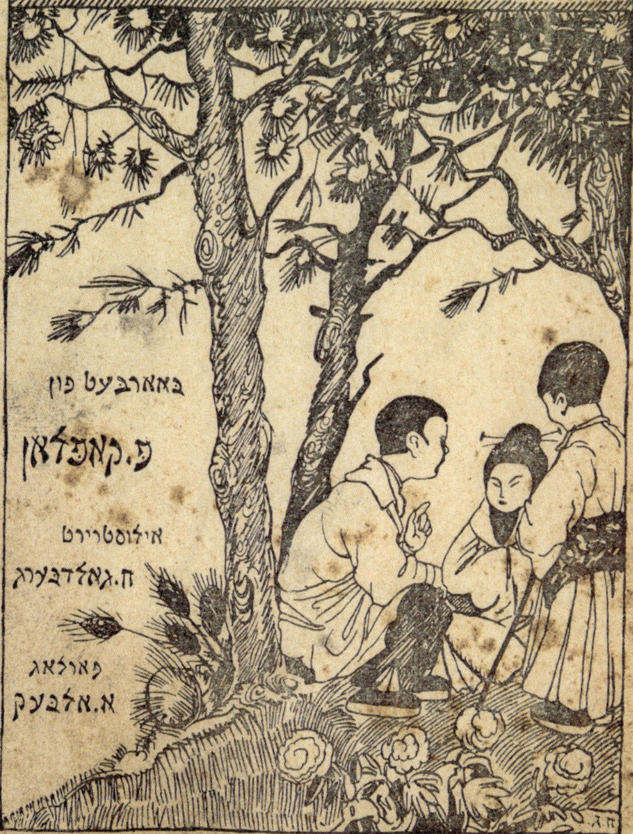

באארבעט פון

פ. קאפלאן

אילוסטרירט

ח. גאלדבערג

פארלאג

א. אלבעק

איבערגעזעצט פון יאפאניש מ. ראקאווסקי.

## A RAYZE TSU DER LEVONE

(A Journey to the Moon)

IDA GLAZER (1891-1947), NEW YORK, 1940

The colorful cover illustration takes its inspiration from the title story in this collection of children's tales. Other pieces include the fantastic and folksy "*A Story with Two Bears*" and "*Journey in a Cloud Ship*." Ida Glazer, who also used the English name Edith Glasser, studied medicine in Utah and journalism at New York University. She also translated the stories of O. Henry into Yiddish.

# אַ רייזע צו דער לבנה

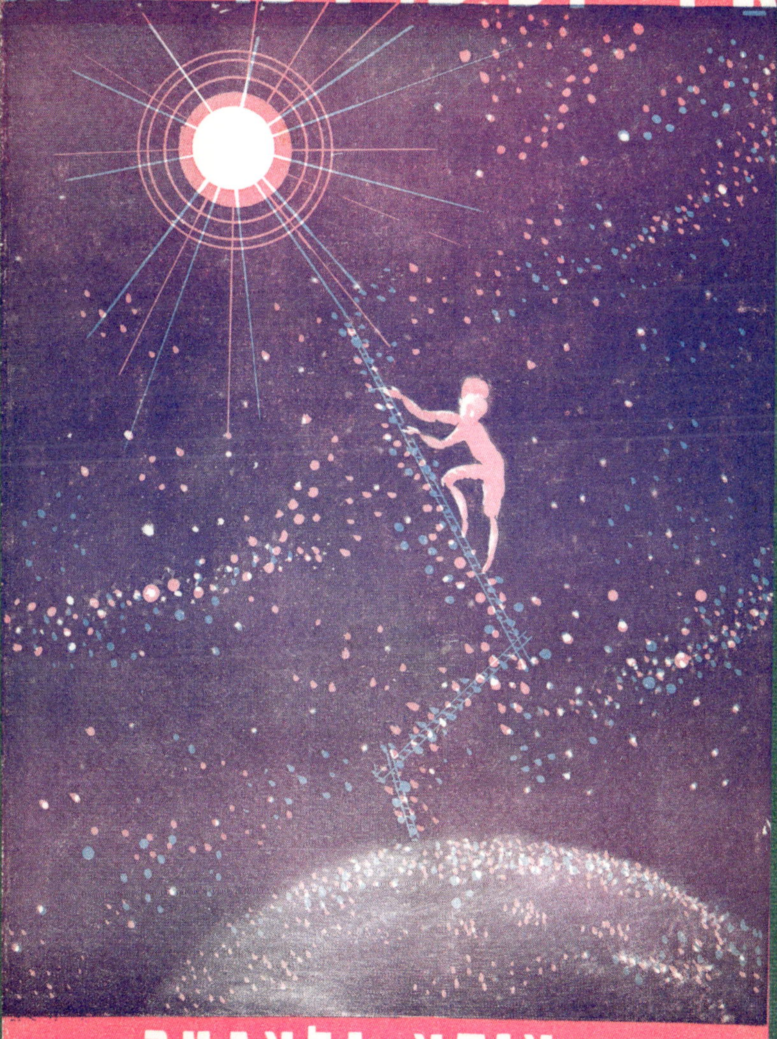

פון אידאַ גלאַזער